D1530469

THE HOW **NOT** TO COOKBOOK

Contents

Burns

Do not burn water. Do not burn the beets dry, do not boil the rhubarb dry—or you will be constantly in the soup over burnt pans!

Always check that elements are switched off—and cool—before placing objects on top of them that you do not want heated, such as tea towels or utensils. Even better, do not put anything on top of an element that would not normally go there.

Do not cook meat on a high flame or it will burn.

Do not ever force open a pressure cooker! And do not ever place your head right above the cover if you were to force open a pressure cooker after cooking. If you do, you can burn your face quite badly.

Do not forget that hot oil and water are major causes of accidents in the kitchen. When handling a pan with hot oil, always keep the grip to the inside of your stove; this way you do not have to worry about accidentally flipping the pan and burning yourself.

Do not forget to place a trivet under a hot pot, especially before setting it on your parents' eighteenth-century table.

Do not heat a pan without anything in it.

Do not microwave already baked or fried plantains, as they have become dehydrated and may begin to smoke.

Do not put a pot with something inside it into a frying pan with oil in it. The steam could go into the oil and make the oil spit and burn you.

Do not put hot pots on the table without a potholder underneath.

Do not think about how nice it would be to have a Rice Pudding, then make one and put it in the oven, forgetting about it until you realize that the smell you can smell and the thought of "how nice it would be to have a rice pudding" are one and the same thing. You will discover the pudding reduced to a black tar in the bottom of the dish.

Do not touch a pot on the stove; even the handle may be scorching!

Do not, in hope of saving time, heat up butter or oil in a pan before you start cutting the vegetables and meat that you want to fry. The oil or butter will probably be burnt before you are finished with the cutting, and you will have to start all over again, with no time saved.

For a Burns Supper do not make deep-fried Bounty Bars if you have already drunk three glasses of wine. There is a high risk of serious injury from hot fat and melted chocolate.

If the risotto sticks to the bottom of your pot, stop stirring and save what is on the top. With a bit of luck the flavor will not be too smoky and you will have stopped your food from having bits of black, burnt crust in it.

If you are going to use Pam or any other aerosol oil, do not spray it on after heating the pan. That type of oil burns really quickly.

If you are very small or quite young, do not try to use a cooker or frying pan without standing on a stool or chair that brings your head well above the level of the pan.

If you are working with hot or boiling water, do not carelessly remove the lid from your pot, steamer, or pressure cooker. Both water and steam are extremely dangerous and can cause severe third-degree burns.

If you burn yourself, do not forget to cut a potato in half and put it on the affected area—the starch will do wonders.

If you have a shockingly short attention span, do not think that burning things has to be the norm. Buy a timer, one that you cannot accidentally turn off when you put it in your pocket.

If you need to taste something that is caramelizing, think twice before you dip your finger into it.

If you pyrolyze oils, you have just created a goopy black carcinogen. Do not try to save it. Throw the whole thing away or pay later on down the line.

If you stir something with a metal implement, never leave it in the pot while it is on the heat. If you do, make sure you use oven gloves to touch it.

Never, EVER try to figure out if you turned on the hotplate by laying your hand on it. The police may wonder why you do not have fingerprints anymore.

On Sunday morning, do not try to pry out that yummy little piece of toast from the toaster using the butter knife. You could end up toasted yourself.

Only cook Turducken outdoors with plenty of space to run if the huge pot of oil is somehow knocked over, spilled, or splashed. It would be a nasty burn!

This might sound obvious, but never use a metal knife to extract your stuck piece of toast from the toaster. If you do, you might get a strong electric shot! When cooking polenta, stir, but do not boil. Polenta bubbles splash and burn when they burst.

When heating oil in a pan, do not forget to make sure the pan is completely dry. Otherwise when the oil gets hot, the water will cause the oil to pop, and it can really burn you.

When living in a vegetarian, nonsmoking collective household, do not try to eat a truly disastrous casserole cooked by a roommate on his designated night to cook dinner for everyone. Do not let the roommate combine his mixture of vegetables with a pound of uncooked noodles. What will come out an hour later will be a crunchy, inedible pile of dry, burnt noodles mixed with dried-out vegetables, leaving you with an inedible dinner and ten empty bellies that evening. When in doubt, always cook the noodles first.

When working with hot sugar or caramel, avoid any contact with your skin. If you burn yourself DO NOT try to remove the caramel. You will probably take a piece of skin with it. Just place the affected area under cold water and wait until it dissolves.

Bread

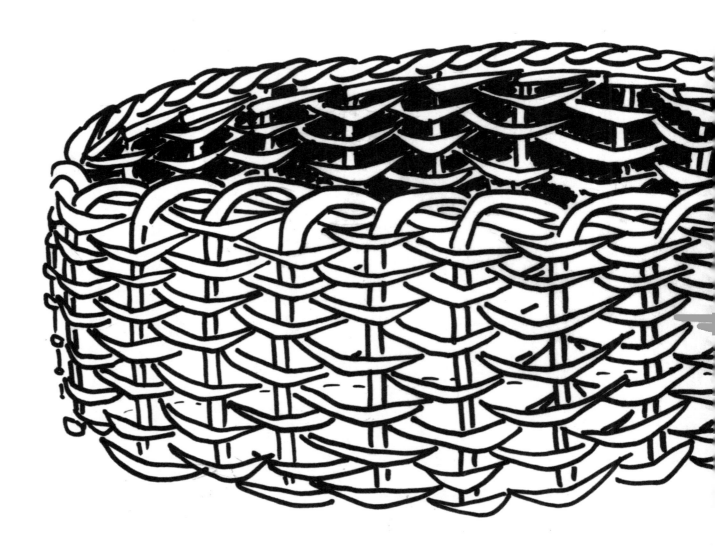

A cucumber is a poor substitute when making zucchini bread, no matter how similar they appear.

Do not refrigerate bread.

Do not buy breadcrumbs at a supermarket. They are processed in a factory, and are therefore much too fine. Make the breadcrumbs yourself or buy them in a bakery. The texture is coarser and better for frying.

Do not fully submerge your stuffing in water or broth before baking it. By the time the liquid cooks out of it, it will have turned into a floppy goo.

Do not serve bread during Passover—especially whole wheat.

Do not throw away your stale bread. You can turn it into breadcrumbs or soften it in the microwave.

Do not throw out bread. It can be used for breadcrumbs.

Do not make breadcrumbs from rye bread. It will never work.

When preparing bread, time is important. If you are in a rush or are just plain lazy and you do not knead properly or let the dough stand for the necessary time needed, the bread will come out with the thickness of a bamboo flute and it will surely break one or more of your teeth.

Do not waste your time going through the whole process of mixing, kneading, and baking bread when you do not know what lukewarm is really supposed to mean. When the water is too hot, you will kill your yeast and end up using your hard-as-rock boule as a doorstop.

If the baguette you bought yesterday is hard, do not throw it away! Rub some tap water over the surface and put it in the oven for a few minutes. If you still have leftovers after that, save it and make a bread pudding, croutons, or breadcrumbs.

If you are trying to be a Bedouin and want to prepare your very own sand-baked bread like they do in the desert, go to the next sandbox in your neighborhood, prepare a fire in the sand, place dough consisting of flour, salt, and water on the fire-bed, and cover with ash from the fire along with sand. Be aware you might step in dog poo.

Just after setting the mix for making bread, do not accompany your wife on a brief shopping trip. Four hours later, you may come home to find that the load has collapsed and cannot be revived. Do not try baking it—it will be inedible! Do not be talked into short trips when preparing bread.

Never eat pasta with bread.

When baking bread on top of a woodstove, never use a nonstick cake baking pan. It becomes too hot and sticks and burns.

When buying bread that is still hot, do not completely close the paper bag or the condensation vapors will moisten the bread and it will lose its aroma.

When rolling out dough, do not roll back and forth over the same section. Rolling out from the center is okay. Rolling back and forth will cause the baked dough to be the texture of cardboard.

When working with dough, do not flour your hands. To prevent dough from sticking, flour your working table and pour some oil or butter over your hands.

Whenever you use flour, do not expect it to be only in the places you want it to be, especially during bread production.

Your biscuits will come out tough if you handle the dough too much. Do not overmix.

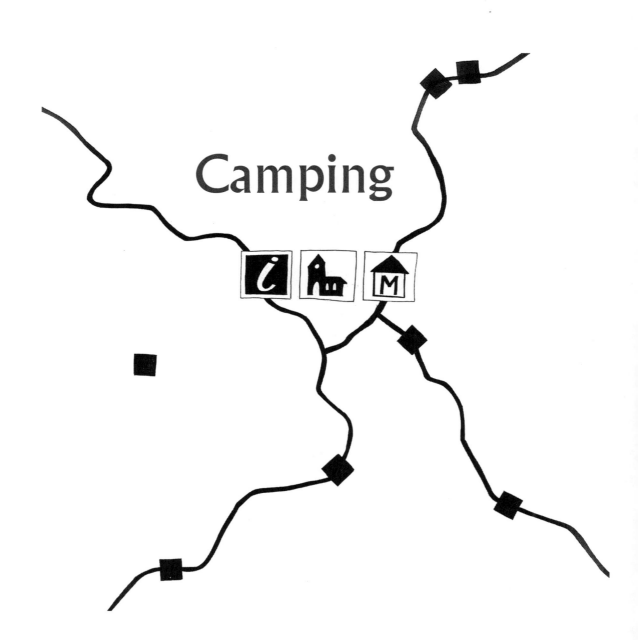

Camping

Do not attempt to cook raw egg in a pie-iron oven on a campfire at 2 a.m., because at that hour of the night you will not be patient enough to let it cook through.

When camping in a small tent, remember to puncture any can that you are going to boil on a Primus stove. You do not want to end up in a tent with a beautifully decorated ceiling.

No matter how poor you are, do not eat or cook freeze-dried camping-food hamburgers. Do not force your young children to eat them, or there will be much gagging and spitting out. Then, when the children are in bed, do not also participate in the reconstituted nonsense. The first mouthful will be so disgusting that you will spit it out in the garden. Next time, just eat carrots.

Cheese

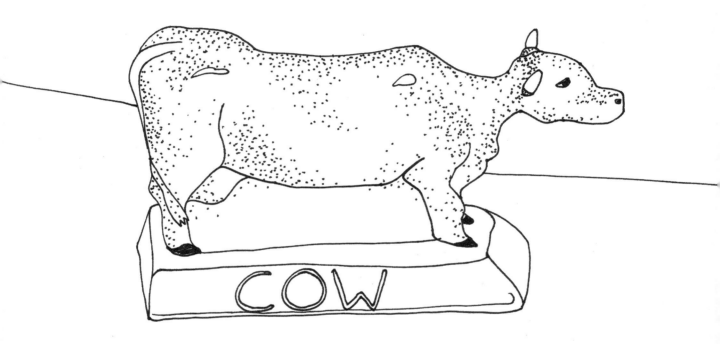

Do not offer blue cheese to people who are not already accomplished with it.

Do not be fooled into thinking that stirring cream cheese (the type normally spread on bagels) into your Tomato and Basil Pasta Sauce will yield the same results as if you used a heavenly mascarpone.

Do not eat cheese directly from the refrigerator. Always let it sit out for a couple of hours before serving.

Do not put cheese on pasta.

Do not try frying mozzarella in your pan unless you have the proper equipment—i.e., a real deep-frying pan and frying oil—even if you just want to make your plastic-tasting mozzarella a little tastier. If you put it in the pan, it will just melt! Do not treat mozzarella like haloumi.

Do not try to make Tarte Siflette with a cheese whose name sounds like Reblochon, whose shape looks like Reblochon, but is not Reblochon. It does not work!

Do not use a plastic spoon to stir cheese sauce. It can melt, and sometimes people do not notice until after they have eaten it.

If you are intending to prepare pasta simply with melted cheese on top it is not advisable to throw mozzarella cheese into boiling water. The cheese will not melt but shrink into a doughy mass resembling old chewing gum.

If you happen upon a large amount of fruit-and-nut-studded cheese, and you do not like it, do not try to make a cheesecake out of it by running it through a food processor with some milk and then baking it. You still will not like it.

If you love cheese but you cannot stand those hard edges after it has been in the fridge, rub some oil on the corners and it will not happen again.

Never freeze fresh cheeses such as mozzarella. When defrosted, the juicy milky center will have disappeared and you will be eating a ball of cheese-flavored ice cream.

Never use cheap cheeses, grated Parmesan in a can, bag, or tin, spray butter or oil, or whipped cream that keeps for more than half a day.

When making Macaroni and Cheese, it is not a good idea to use Edam cheese, even if it is the only thing left in the fridge. It solidifies, and you are left with something you could build a wall with.

When trying to think of something different to add to a stir-fry, do not add cheese. The result will be an unsatisfying solid mass of inedible food.

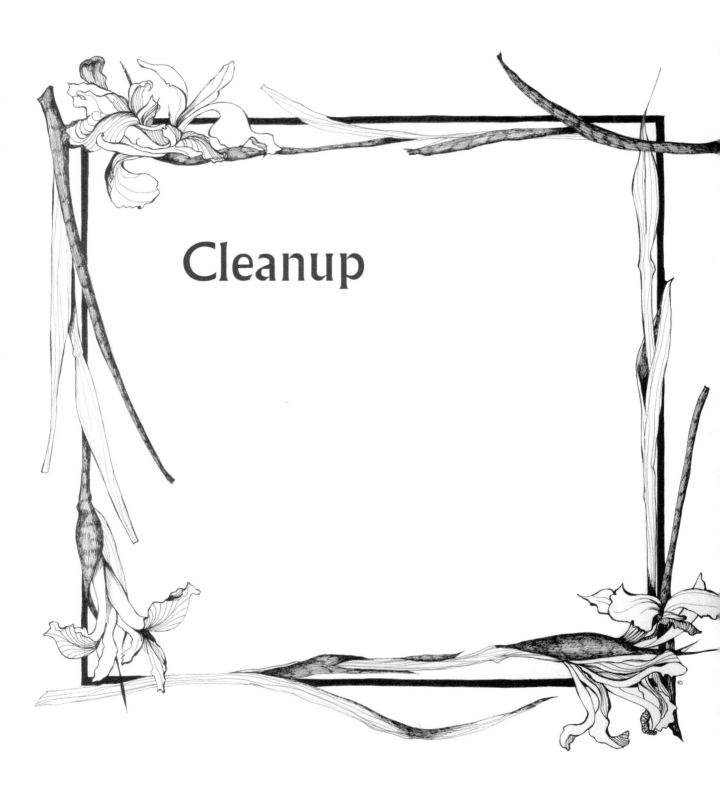

Cleanup

Do not cook if you want a clean kitchen.

Do not add salt to water before it is boiling or it will leave traces almost impossible to remove at the bottom of the pan—no matter how hard you scrub with Brillo pads.

Do not leave wooden spoons in the dishwater.

Do not put chickpeas on to boil and then go down to meet the neighbors for a drink. You will come back to black smoke, hard chickpeas, and a pan that will take a couple of weeks to clean.

Do not stack the plates on top of each other when clearing the table.

Do not throw all of the ingredients to make mayonnaise into a blender. You will not get mayonnaise but a slimy mess instead.

Do not try to cook vegetables and read or do anything else at the same time, as you can be sure that they will burn—heavily. If they do you must fill the pot with vinegar and water, not to the top but just to where the burned part starts.

Do not wash a cutting board with soap or detergent.

Do not wash the caffettiera with soap or detergent.

If you clean the oven, do it properly. If you do not, the next thing you bake in the oven will be steamed in toxic cleaning-cream fog.

Never wash a frying pan. Clean it out with cooking oil and cloth straight after use, while it is still warm, so that it will develop its nonstick properties. This patina gets better and better as a nonstick surface over time. Using abrasion, soap, or water ruins it.

Never wash cast iron with soap! Thoroughly dry a skillet or Dutch oven, and apply oil after each use.

Never wash your pans with soap and water; otherwise you will wash away all of the yummy flavors of your previous dishes.

When making caramel by placing a can of condensed milk in boiling water do not let the pot boil dry. It takes several days to scrape the congealed caramel off the ceiling and walls.

When making sauce, never put fresh tomatoes in a pan filled with hot oil. If you love your kitchen!

When trying to make your first ever Banoffee Pie, do not go outside and lie in the sun while boiling a can of condensed milk. If you do you will only return a couple of hours later to find the kitchen completely covered in toffee sauce. Needless to say, you will spend the next year cleaning up the mess.

Coffee

When you live by yourself, you need only enough water for one.

When using a classic Italian napolitana for your coffee, never use soap to wash it. Otherwise your next coffee will smell like a bubble bath.

Do not forget to put the water in the caffettiera or the caffettiera will explode.

Do not leave coffee for too long in a metal caffettiera; it will rust quickly.

Do not put too much coffee in the caffettiera or it will explode!

Do not put too much coffee in the caffettiera; the coffee will taste too strong.

Never put the coffee maker on without filling it with water first.

Do not rush a French press.

Do not wash your coffee pot. Period. People think that washing their coffee makers and presses is a regular thing to do, just like you wash anything else. But certain things like coffee makers and nonstick pans do not need to be cleaned that way. Just rinse your coffee maker, pot, or French press with regular tap water. This way you will leave all the coffee oils in the pot and you will actually enjoy a more flavorful cup of coffee. If you are a clean freak, just run some vinegar mixed with hot water through your coffee maker once a month, but never, ever use dishwashing liquid.

When using a stovetop coffee pot, check and double-check that you have closed the valve properly. If you do not, this will result in a terrible shock for everyone, frightened cats, and an urgent need to redecorate your kitchen. Oh, and worst of all, no coffee.

If you want to make Lapacho tea, never use an aluminum pot for boiling. The aluminum destroys all benefits of the Lapacho. Always use stainless steel or glass. The same for storing the tea.

When making spicy chai, do not add more hot spices such as pepper and anise than sweet ones such as cardamom and cloves, or the drink will lose its comforting qualities.

Do not fill the kettle all the way to the top with water, as it takes too long to boil and wastes energy.

Cover-up

When cooking a good TV dinner, make sure you read carefully whether the film is supposed to come off or stay on before you pop it in the microwave.

Do not underestimate the importance of mastering the lid. It is a big part of cooking. Use it whenever you want to cook something all the way through, without waiting too long; for example, when frying an egg. Turn the stove to high so that you have a very hot surface, break the egg, lower the heat to medium, and then put the lid on. You will enjoy a perfect white and yellow fried egg with no transparent raw yolk on top.

Never cover the pan when frying.

Do not dry-roast mustard seeds without having a pan lid on hand. They pop and jump when heated.

Do not be impatient when cooking veal liver. Do not hasten the cooking time by turning up the flame and do not take the cover off the pan before the very last few seconds. It will harden and burn and taste miserable.

Do not boil water without using a lid on your pot—your gas bill will thank you for it.

Do not forget to fix the lid on your blender, or your kitchen will turn into a colorful liquid mess.

During your student days you and your friend may decide to make some popcorn by heating a little oil in a pan, putting the dry kernels in, and then waiting for the popping to start. After the initial excitement of watching the tiny pieces burst into popcorn shapes you will be taken aback as pieces start to escape from the pan, jumping into the air. You will huddle together screaming as the pieces ricochet off the walls. Eventually you will sweep up the dusty nuggets and feed them to your roommate.

If you are looking for an oven alternative to baked frozen pizza because your oven is toxic, do not try to steam the pizza in a pot. It will not taste good.

If you do not want to use a timer and do not want to have a disaster in the kitchen try the African technique. Take the food off the flame and place it on a spot with a thick bit of felted wool fabric on the counter, then drape with a kitchen towel, your down jacket, a lap blanket, or an old malleable cat that appreciates free warmth. The food will continue to cook but you will save fuel, energy, and money.

If you need to flip something you are frying, flip it toward yourself. And if you are not sure you can pull it off, but you still need to flip it, help yourself with a plate or a lid.

When and if the oil is burning never use water to put it out. Use a pan cover.

When boiling escargots, do not leave the pot uncovered. Cover the pot with a lid to prevent them from escaping their boiling death. Do the same with any other animal you cook alive, like crab and lobster.

When cooking rice, do not take the lid off.

When you are given food in the hospital, remember to check to see if there is any plastic wrap covering the meal—you do not want to be accused of going blind.

When making popcorn, when you put the kernels into the pot never forget to cover it or you will find your kitchen covered in little crunchy balls.

Dating

It may seem macho to use a hand whisk in place of an electric mixer, but do not be tempted, especially when the recipe says to whisk for fifteen minutes. She will not be impressed and you will look like a fool.

When cooking a Cheese Fondue in a small kitchen, do not put the wine on the heat and then go off to get ready for your party with your best friend without either opening the window or checking on the concoction from time to time. When you return to the kitchen, you will find it so filled with alcoholic smog that neither of you will be able to make it to the cooker or window without getting high on the fumes. While the eventual dish can still be rescued and enjoyed by your guests, the state of your hair, makeup, and general demeanor will be quite beyond repair and your bemused guests will not understand your sustained giggliness at all. This is particularly important if you are trying to impress a potential new partner with this dish. You will not.

If you are preparing a very romantic dinner, with a very sophisticated menu, for the first time in order to impress your date, do not buy two big, beautiful artichokes at the market unless you are aware of the fact that they are supposed to be cooked. Do not serve them raw.

If you have invited your latest flame to dinner and you want to make them Seafood Spaghetti, do not forget to check each and every clam. Sand is not much of an aphrodisiac.

If you have planned to impress your date by cooking pasta with prawns and you forget the cream, do not add milk instead. Slimy lumps of curdled protein in an otherwise thin and tasteless sauce will be the result—and an indignant-looking girl on the other side of the table.

If you want to feed your date by cooking tomatoes mixed with eggs, take into account that after adding butter and oil do not also add a jar of peanut butter. She will not feel like having sex after eating this.

Never allow your university-educated girlfriend to boil water in a plastic cup on an electric cooker ring. It will melt the cup and cause a bad smoke to fill the tiny apartment. If this happens, do not ask pointless questions like: "Why did you boil water in a plastic cup? Didn't you know it would melt?" Henceforth, be suspicious of all educated people in general.

When cooking with your boyfriend, do not forget to make it clear who is the chef in advance. If not you might end up fighting and lose your appetite.

When making the Northeast delicacy Garlic Stottie, do not use raw garlic paste. It is better to melt some softly browned garlic with butter. The resulting side dish will go spankingly well with lasagna and will easily win you a place in a Geordie's heart.

When your son invites his girlfriend over for the first time, try not to cook something fairly unconventional. It should be noted that pig's tails are not conventional and may cause an uncomfortable half-hour silence while she pokes a single boiled potato with her fork before excusing herself from the dinner table.

Defrosting

When defrosting green beans, never put them directly into boiling water—they will be transformed into lead bullets for hunting.

Do not defrost bread in the microwave.

Do not get irritated by how long things take to defrost in the microwave on the defrost setting and then turn it up to full power—even for thirty seconds. You will end up with a half-cooked, melted, or rubbery mess.

Do not use a microwave to defrost your frozen food. When you use the stove or the oven, the heat is transferred to the food from the inside out, while if you use a microwave the heat goes from the outside in, so your food will look cooked on the edges but will probably still be frosted and raw. The waves deform the molecular structure of food and remove a bunch of nutrients and minerals from it, leaving it a weird, dry, bubble-gum texture.

Never put fish in your freezer in a developing country and go away on vacation for a month not realizing that there will be a power cut while you are gone. The stench of rotten fish will never leave your freezer, no matter how much baking soda or activated charcoal you put in there. You will have to buy a new freezer.

Dessert

When making coconut cake, do not leave out the coconut.

Do not attempt to make a meringue. It will always burn.

Unless you want to make butter, do not whip the cream for too long.

Oh, my God, never confuse plastic food trays with cookie sheets! Baking casualty!

Do not forget the rising agent in your sponge cake. It will be more like a cookie than a cake. If you try to feed it to the birds, they will sense that they would not lift off the ground so even they will turn their beaks up at it!

Beware of messy meringues. Having enjoyed a Hazelnut Meringue Roulade at a friend's, you may ask for the recipe. However, when you cook the dish, the meringue will spread over the sides of the Swiss roll pan and cover the bottom of the oven. It will take forever to clean up, but you might be able to salvage what was left of the pan.

Do not add walnuts to your brownie batter. It adds unnecessary heaviness to an already heavy treat.

Do not bake brownies in a toaster oven—they will catch on fire!

Do not be discouraged if you have trouble making cakes and find that the middle is often soggy. Use a ring-shaped cake pan instead.

Do not blend fat with liquid when making pastries. Flour must be cut with fat, then the liquids blended in.

Do not forget the sugar when you are making your chocolate cake. Oh, God, how bad it tastes without the sugar!

Do not forget to add flour to a cake unless you are planning to make mousse.

Do not make a Christmas log. They never look good.

Do not mix the ingredients of a chocolate mousse with a wooden spoon. The egg whites will turn into liquid.

Do not overwhip cream; it will only end up looking cheap and tacky.

Do not overheat your wonderful Zabaglione or you will have nothing but sweet scrambled eggs.

Do not remove your cake, cupcakes, or muffins from their mold until they are completely cold. If you do it while they are still hot they will break.

Do not spit in the pudding. If you do, the starch will be separated from the milk.

Do not start making a pie when your guests are coming in an hour.

Do not stir chocolate until it is entirely melted. Otherwise you stop the melting process and it will become opaque.

Do not substitute white sugar for brown sugar in cookie recipes. While the resulting taste might not be that much different, brown sugar makes cookies soft and chewy inside and white sugar makes them hard and crisp.

Do not think that store-bought cakes are the same as homemade ones. They never will be.

Do not try to make food scary for Halloween. Lychees dyed black will turn the ice cream gray and will never be desired.

Do not try to make a pie for the first time unsupervised.

Do not try to recycle failed cakes into Trifle; they can remain heavy and lumpy even when soaked in alcohol.

Do not whip cream too much. The stage which follows whipped is forever unwhipped.

For Pan d'Arancio, never put fresh orange juice in the recipe. Always use orange extract.

If after adding egg yolks, bars of chocolate, and blocks of butter, the recipe then calls for melting the ingredients in a bain-marie, do not use a springform cake pan. The water will seep in and turn your indulgent chocolate cake into chocolate soup.

If you are making a rather gooey and deliciously indulgent chocolate cake, due to all of the rich extra butter and sugar included, it may not rise to perfection. You will be left with a tremendously tall chocolate cake with a crater the size of Vesuvius in the center. (You can still turn this disaster around. Shake confectioners' sugar over the collapsed cake and add a little skiing figure and some trees. Not only is it still a delicious cake but it will look like an intentional feature!)

If you are making brownies, be careful not to overbake them. They get dry and crumbly and lose all their moist chewiness. It is better that they are a little bit underbaked than overbaked.

If you are melting chocolate do not let a single drop of water fall into it. If this happens, it will be lumpy forever.

When taking the Carrot Cake out of the oven, do not let it get completely cold before taking it out of the baking pan. This will cause the cake stick to the pan, and you may end up scraping half of the cake out with a fork.

If you want to make cookies and you are out of parchment paper, do not just put the cookies on the oven's grate. They will melt.

Never mix the ingredients of a chocolate mousse with a wooden spoon; the egg white will turn into liquid.

Never put a cake to cook on the lowest rack in the oven. When you turn it out of the mold the bottom will probably be burnt.

Never whip cream in a warm bowl or a bowl sitting on a warm surface; it will take you ages to get it whipped.

No matter how tempting it is to open the oven door while baking a nice sponge cake, do not do it or your cake will sag and droop in the middle—very upsetting.

Once it is cooked, do not leave a cake in the oven even if it has been switched off. It will get dry.

Read the instructions on how to make buttercream. Do not freestyle and mash a block of butter and a bag of sugar together.

When baking a cake, make sure that the oven is at the right temperature for the entire baking time; otherwise the cake will come out hard.

When baking a cake that uses a layer of toffee, make sure the toffee layer is not too thick. Even if you make a beautiful cake with a very professional toffee layer, it will be less impressive if you have to use a hammer and chisel to break through the topping to release the cake.

When baking a cake, always double-check whether your flour contains rising agent or whether you have to add it yourself. If in doubt, dip your finger into the flour and taste it. Self-rising flour will taste slightly salty, while plain flour is tasteless. A cake baked without baking powder only makes for a very good doorstop, so do not forget to add it!

When baking a cake, do not overwhisk your eggs.

When baking a cake, do not trip up at the final hurdle. A little trick for making sure your cake comes out of the pan nicely is to sprinkle it with a little flour first.

When baking a cake, NEVER open the oven. The mix will go flat and your cake will not be properly cooked. This is the reason oven lights were invented, so do not open the oven door even if you are dying to see how your cake is doing. Just follow the recipe and wait.

When blind baking a piecrust, never forget to line the crust with parchment paper before you fill it with rice or dry beans. Otherwise you will end up with a disaster when the rice or beans cook into the pastry and the whole thing has to be thrown out.

When cooking with chocolate, do not forget to double the quantities of any cocoa-based products needed for the recipe. This takes into consideration the one piece for you and one piece for the mixing bowl policy, which must always be adhered to when cooking with such tasty ingredients.

When making caramel you need sugar and butter. Do not use sugar alone or it will turn black very quickly. A burned smell will ruin your thrill of anticipation.

When making chocolate cake and the recipe calls for four egg whites and two yolks, do not use six eggs. You only need four.

After making a Chocolate-Coated Zabaglione Mousse in a round ring mold, do not remove the mold from the freezer and warm it with a hot towel. Do not invert and give it a tap. Do not reheat the towel and re-tap harder. Do not tell your child to get his little wooden mallet. Do not reheat the mold and start banging, because the mold dents and shakes but the chocolate clings tightly and the zabaglione will start melting. Guests will be doubled up with laughter, and the air in the kitchen will be bright blue. The children will be thrilled to hear all those words coming out of your mouth.

When making cream pies, do not forget that the crust should be baked in advance. There is very little recourse once the pastry shell has been filled.

When making crumble, do not forget to crumble the flour and butter together before you put them on the fruit.

When making custard, do not underestimate the importance of doing so in a bowl over simmering water. Using a pan directly on the heat will result in a dish that resembles watery and sweetened scrambled eggs.

When using confectioners' sugar, do not add too much water, lemon juice, or flavoring to it or you will be left with a runny, gooey mixture. To rectify the mishap, add more confectioners' sugar and keep stirring until you have icing thick enough to cement bricks together.

When you are icing a cake, add a wee amount of water bit by bit, otherwise you will have the wrong consistency.

When making Apple Strudel, neither flatten the dough too much nor leave it too thick.

When preparing Strawberry Dessert, do not add too much water to the boiling strawberries; instead add a very little amount of water with sugar and a big amount of strawberries, so the syrup can be considerably more sweet and flavorful.

When making instant cake, do not mix up the bags labeled "cake mix" and "icing." The results will simply be weird.

When finishing a pie or a sweet dessert rich in cream or chocolate, do not hide it as a surprise for your guests by putting it close to the window or leaving it outside. The only surprise for your guests will be the strange optical effect of an uninvited gathering of ants.

Do not add water to sugar when you want to make caramel. It will only take more time, since the water has to evaporate before the chemical reaction happens. Simply put some sugar on a pan and wait until it melts. You do not even have to stir it before it gets lightly brown.

Do not forget baking powder in your cake recipes! If you forget, it will not rise.

If you add too much baking powder or baking soda to your baked goods the results are bittersweet.

Mashed potatoes should not be the chief ingredient in cake. Unless you like gummy cake.

No matter how much you want cake, do not try to flip it out of the pan before it is cooled for a good twenty minutes after leaving the oven. Definitely do not try to flip it out by shaking the pan upside down half a foot above your cooling rack or plate.

Unless you are an expert, never put gum thickener in your muffins.

When making custard, let hot liquids cool a little before adding them to egg yolks. If you do not, you will have scrambled eggs!

When making flan for the first time, do not think you have made a mistake when the sugar hardens in the custard cups and then proceed to boil the cups in water to remove the hardened sugar. You will realize later that the sugar is softened when the custard is baked.

When you are icing a cake around other people, do not lick the spatula before you have finished. Someone will see.

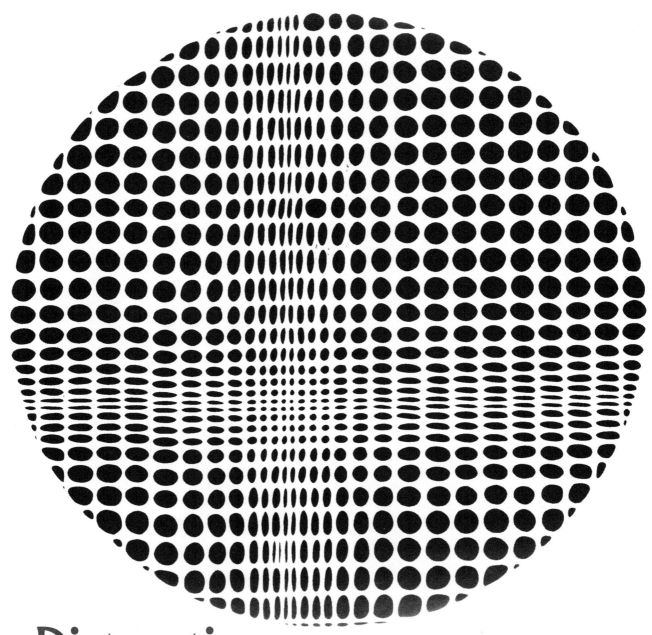

Distraction

Do not answer the phone while frying bacon.

Do not read a book when you are cooking. It is distracting.

Do not answer the telephone while you are cooking. It is a distraction that can amount to cooking disasters.

Do not ask a young doctor doing his or her residency to cook dinner. They will always be in a rush, and the food will never be good.

Do not ask an artist to cook for you when they are busy.

Do not be on the phone while cooking or eating. It will give you a bad neck pain later.

Do not cook when you are in a rush.

Do not cook while you are watching the news or thinking about problems. Just think about what you are going to eat!

Do not daydream in the kitchen. You need to be awake to make food.

Do not disturb the chef before Easter.

Do not fall asleep while cooking.

Do not fry an egg while you have an original-language version of a Kurosawa film playing in the living room. It is not a good idea.

Do not get distracted when making French Toast and use cayenne pepper instead of cinnamon.

Do not walk away when you are cooking something.

Do not instant message on Facebook while cutting garlic.

Do not place mustard next to your toothpaste if you like to watch TV while cooking.

Do not talk on the telephone while cooking!

Do not watch films with a stew in the oven if your mother is in the hospital, unless you have a timer on it. The stew will be burnt to a crisp.

Do not watch TV while cooking.

If friends are visiting for the weekend and you spend the day horse riding, do not preset your oven timer to cook a full roast chicken dinner and then put chicken in the wrong oven.

If most of your kitchen disasters arise from lack of attention that stems from growing up with a mother who could burn boiled eggs, do not forget that the best solution is a small investment in a kitchen timer.

If you are cooking eggs for breakfast, do not put the extra-virgin olive oil in the frying pan and then go outside to putter in the garden, as this distraction can lead to a smoky and smelly kitchen and feelings of doom narrowly avoided.

Less is more, so do not make things complicated—do not cook in a rush.

Making caramel in a pan requires your full attention. After you put the butter and sugar in the pan, make sure to keep stirring. Do not check your email, clean away the dishes, or do anything else. Otherwise the smoke in the air will tell you that you can forget about the caramel and the pan as well.

Never leave a pan of potatoes cooking and leave the house.

Never walk away from something that is on the stove. An espresso pot is easily destroyed, the plastic handle melted, the gasket annihilated.

A pot of covered beans unattended will rattle and shake, spitting hot water everywhere. You may be in another room crediting the neighbors with the racket, but it is your problem and eventually your scorched beans and ruined pan too!

The secret to the kitchen, so vegetables do not overcook, bread does not burn, meat does not dry out, pasta is not overdone, and the rice does not smash, is not to talk on the phone or do something else while cooking; in other words, do not forget to concentrate.

When having friends over for lunch, do not go for a walk after putting your vegetables and meat in the oven, especially if the oven is on auto.

While boiling spaghetti water, do not start two parallel chats on Facebook.

When you cook, do not leave until it is done.

Do not try to cook when you are stoned. It gives you paranoia.

It is not a good idea to smoke while you are cooking. The ash could end up in the frying pan and the salt in the ashtray.

Do not cook in a rush or while you are high because you will end up eating disgusting things, cutting yourself, or throwing your entire meal into the trash for no reason. Focus!

Do not drink and cook. Taste buds and portions are distorted when you are slightly drunk.

Do not permit your teenage son or daughter to stuff your Christmas turkey. Many hours later and exhausted from feasting and laughing, you will at last notice two black cats draped across the dinner table. They will remain there, unconscious and floppy until they wake up twenty-four hours later, refreshed and frisky. You might discover that it was not sage and oregano that went into that turkey's belly; it may be some other herb your child has been cultivating in the backyard. Lessons: (1) grow your own herbs, (2) take responsibility for maintaining yuletide standards, (3) only keep vegetarian pets, and (4) never waste good ganja on dead birds—unless you want a particularly pleasant and languid festive season.

Do not think that everything tastes better with a little sip of alcohol.

Do not try to make microwaveable popcorn after many pints without reading the instructions. If you do, it will result in smoke residue in your microwave, your microwave vent, and the walls and windows of your apartment or house.

Take care cooking when you are on heavy medications. You might fall asleep before eating. Upon waking up you might find your meal in your combo-microwave, only to then fall asleep again and forget about it for five weeks.

Eggs

When boiling an egg, please do not follow a Catholic mother's advice to repeat three Our Father prayers in a row until they are ready. Just simmer for ten to fifteen minutes. If you do it the Catholic way you will get green yolks.

Do not eat soft-boiled eggs with a silver spoon. They will stain the spoon and taste bad.

When you are making a soufflé, do not open the oven before it is done.

Do not assume your egg whites will form stiff peaks when you beat them, unless your bowls are really clean.

Be extra-careful not to burn scrambled eggs if you have a hangover. It is a particularly horrible smell.

Do not ask a blonde to cook a soft-boiled egg!

Do not ask how it is possible to cook four eggs simultaneously for the same length of time and end up with two hard-boiled ones and two raw ones. If you have achieved this disaster of a breakfast, accept that you will never be any sort of a cook and offer to do the washing up instead.

Do not break an egg directly into whatever you are cooking—first break the egg into a cup or a bowl. The egg could be bad and can ruin your dish.

Do not crack eggshells directly into the ingredients. It is best to crack eggshells into a cup before adding to the rest of the ingredients to avoid stray eggshell particles.

Do not forget about boiling eggs. They will turn into sulfur bombs.

Do not forget to add bicarbonate to your Frittata—if you want a fluffy Frittata.

Do not leave an egg boiling in the saucepan and then go off to church. Not a good idea! The stench of an overcooked exploded egg is not worth it.

Do not mix egg whites and egg yolks when cooking anything. It just does not work.

Do not mix your whisked egg whites until they get completely hard. They reach their full-blown potential when they are a little creamy. Do not try to turn the mixing bowl upside down over your head to check if they are hard or sticky enough.

Do not open the oven when cooking a soufflé.

Do not overboil eggs. The longer an egg boils, the more sulfur is released from the eggshell.

Do not overcook scrambled eggs; they will lose their buttery softness.

Do not put your eggs in the fridge. They are better at room temperature unless you live in a hot place.

Do not think you can make a very good soufflé with flour and tomato juice.

Egg Fried Pasta is a made-up dish and tastes better without the egg.

Follow grandmother's advice: Do not break eggs into an empty bowl. Before breaking eggs you should place them in a bowl of water. The rotten eggs will float and the fresh ones will sink.

For boiling an egg, do not try to press it through the spout of the kettle. Use a small pot instead.

If you are poor, do not forget that a Fritatta Romana is filling and cheap to make.

If you make an omelette and add ten egg whites but do not add egg yolks, you may find it to be a rather bland and depressing meal, particularly when eaten on its own, with no sauce.

If your recipe uses a lot of eggs, do not break them all in the same bowl; instead break them in a separate bowl just in case one of them is rotten so that you do not waste your whole recipe.

Make sure to add vinegar and salt to the water when poaching eggs. If you do not, your eggs will not be poached.

Never cook with eggs that you have just taken out of the fridge. Whatever you need to do with them, it is a good idea for them to be at room temperature.

Never put your egg whites in the fridge before whipping. Cold egg whites will not rise.

Never use metal utensils with a frying pan. If you do, your omelette will stick.

Soufflé is not complicated, really, but you have to stick to the recipe, and if the recipe says that the eggs should be firm, then they have to be firm. Soupy eggs will turn your soufflé into a weird liquid quiche. Once you have placed your mix in the soufflé mold, do not slam the oven door shut. Instead, close the oven door gently so that you do not burst all the bubbles on top of your soufflé.

To make hard-boiled eggs, do not put the eggs into a pot of water already boiling.

When boiling an egg, do not put the cold egg in the hot water. Let the egg heat up in the water. If it does not heat up with the temperature of the heating water the egg will crack and trail gross little egg tentacles all around the pot of water.

When boiling an egg, make sure the pot does not boil dry. As well as not ruining the pot, this will help you to avoid a truly awful, all-pervading smell which lingers for weeks.

When frying eggs over-easy, do not flip them until the bottom of the yolk has hardened; otherwise the yolk will break and ruin the presentation.

When making a frittata, never use a high flame and too much oil.

When making a savory quiche or flan, do not be tempted to use a readymade sweetened pastry crust—the result will be appalling.

When making frittata with potatoes, cook over a low flame. If you use a high flame, the frittata will start to dance in its pan and the outside will burn and the inside will not be cooked.

When poaching an egg, it is an undeniably common misconception that it is necessary to add vinegar to the water. Simply bring water to a simmer and slide the cracked egg into the pot. When cooked to a preference of melty/medium/hard, use a slotted spoon to remove the egg from the water and allow the steam to dissipate. The egg is now perfectly poached. Do not use vinegar in this process because it will ruin the method and taste.

When thickening a soup or sauce with an egg, do not let it boil after adding the egg. It will curdle at once.

When you are making something that requires the addition of eggs to a mixture that may have hot ingredients in it such as melted butter, always let the mixture cool down before adding the eggs. If you do not you will end up with a queasy scrambled mixture and there will never be enough of the right ingredients in your kitchen to repeat the recipe. You will end up having to walk to the store to buy more and possibly spraining your ankle on the way home.

You should not add salt to the egg whites to whip it up. It does not help and the salt can react with the water of the egg whites.

When making Carbonara, be careful not to cook the eggs, because at the end you will have frittata and not Carbonara.

Erotica

Never cook naked. You will get hot fat on your chest and you never know what will happen from behind.

Be careful with erotic tomfoolery in the kitchen; splashes of hot oil can cause very unpleasant chain reactions.

Cooking eight-inch sausages on a BBQ surrounded by a bunch of homosexuals with unlimited free beer is not a good idea—at least not if you are straight.

Do not choke the chicken after having chopped hot peppers.

Do not cook if you are madly in love. At least be careful with salt. It is not a rumor. It is a fact.

Do not cook naked. Hot oil always finds its way to your most sensitive parts, and that can hurt!

Do not fry a sausage when you have a boner.

Do not have sex while your hot potatoes are roasting.

Do not let your sensual pleasures distract you from the food.

It makes one feel almost as glamorous as Nigella Lawson to be swigging a large glass of spiced Merlot while stirring up a romantic meal for two. The whole experience becomes very relaxing—warm and fuzzy. However, do not take such a blasé approach when preparing a Madhur Jaffrey recipe that requires chopped chiles and garlic. Your lover may arrive while your hands are covered in spices and before you know it you will both have burning crotches, and no amount of scrubbing will get that smell of garlic out!

If you are about to prepare Beef Roulades for the first time in your life, send your partner out of the house. Or at least do not let yourself be seduced into forgetting about time and place. Do not close the door to the bedroom behind you. Otherwise you may remember your Roulades only when they have shrunken into tiny rolls of inedible dark substance. A couple of weeks later you might learn where the double meaning of "having a bun in the oven" comes from.

If you have been cutting chiles for a Thai Curry for your girlfriend, remember to give your hands a good wash before you start any bedroom athletics.

Explosions

KABOOM!!

Take care when lighting a gas oven. You may nearly blow your head off.

Do not put a Pyrex dish that has just come out of the oven onto a marble worktop. It will break.

A reasonable substitute for caramel can be obtained by boiling an unopened can of condensed milk in a pan of water over low heat. Do not allow the pan to boil dry overnight, as the detonation is likely to awaken you quite abruptly.

Do not broil a pork roast in a glass pan. It will explode in the high temperature—the glass, not the pork!

Do not empty a hot saucepan of Lamb Curry straight off the stove into a cold Pyrex dish so that you can keep it warm in the oven. There is a very good chance that it will explode.

Do not forget that the worst experiences in the kitchen often come from the enthusiasm of a pioneer.

Why has no one cooked a whole egg on a barbeque? Because it transforms into an incandescent bomb that with a touch of the spoon will explode violently in your face, hurting you badly.

Do not forget to be very careful when making Uova alla Monachella, because the film that is created between the yolk and the external part of the egg can explode on your face!

Do not heat a plastic jar of honey in a microwave for more than a minute. Even a minute is too long.

Do not heat up leftover soup in a glass jar over a gas flame because the glass will shatter and the food will cover the stovetop.

Do not improvise with a blowtorch instead of using a grill. It works okay with naan breads, but with pizza the toppings will end up on the wall.

Do not look into a gas oven too fast after opening the door. Especially while wearing mascara—it will make your eyelashes glue together.

Do not put metal in the microwave.

Do not put metal or aluminum in the microwave.

Do not try to boil an egg in the microwave. The egg yolk will heat up faster than the egg white and the egg will explode. It is not dangerous, but very unpleasant to clean the microwave afterward.

Do not use gas when drunk. There is always the assumption as a student that, no matter how much beer you have drunk, a couple of slices of toast will cure the hangover. The person most able to stand upright is usually dispatched to the kitchenette to feed the others with toast. If you are on duty, and drunkenly click the lighter, shouting, "The grill seems to be broken," the reply will most likely be, "Keep trying, we need toast," followed by a loud BOOM as the oven door shoots across the room into the wall. You might realize you have turned on the oven instead of the grill!

Hot non-Pyrex glass will shatter when placed on a cold surface.

If you have a gas stove, do not turn on the stove before lighting your match first.

Never, ever put aluminum foil on top of a bowl about to be warmed up in a microwave unless you fancy smoke, electric sparks, and a black microwave.

Never microwave chocolate. At first it will bubble and then turn into a molten ooze. Billows of smoke will fill the air and it will almost immediately turn into ashes—as if it were a victim of an A-bomb explosion.

Never put a pan into a microwave. It sounds like popping corn and produces pretty sparks, but it is highly toxic.

Never put a plastic container into an oven or microwave without verifying whether it is heatproof. The artistic effect is surprising but the smell is terrible.

Never put water into hot oil. It explodes.

When baking something in the oven, make sure you use an ovenproof dish. If you do not you are likely to end up with a big explosion and glass shards in the food.

When cooking a baked potato the good old-fashioned way in the oven, it is a really good idea to remember to stab it several times with a fork first. If you do not, your otherwise peaceful evening will be interrupted by a loud explosion and instead of eating baked potato you will be scraping it off your oven for a while.

When cooking risotto, do not be clever by inventing a shortcut like putting all the ingredients in a Pyrex dish and gently warming it on the gas stove before putting the dish in the oven and then walking away for twenty minutes. The Pyrex will get too hot and will explode. Risotto will go everywhere and little bits of glass will fly through your white T-shirt and cut your tummy. While it might look sort of arty with all those little spots of blood it is not fun and the dinner is ruined. So, open flame + Pyrex = ouch. That is science, and you cannot argue with science.

When oven-baking a pizza for friends, make sure to light the oven after turning the gas on before leaving the room. Otherwise, when you return to place your pizza in the said preheated oven, you will open the door, realize it is not lit, and upon instinct hit the spark switch, you will lose all facial hair, cause a "whooompfhhhh" noise that is felt throughout your block of apartments, and you will be teased for this forever more.

When Pasta and Tuna Gratin is in your oven and you have just learned that one of your guests is allergic to fish, do not put last night's fantastic meat casserole in a glass ovenproof dish, straight from the fridge, onto a fully heated stove. The dish will break with a big sound effect, and your allergic guest will keep searching for glass bits on his plate for the rest of the evening.

When you heat up a Pop Tart in the microwave, make sure to take it out of the wrapper. If you do not, you will have a fireworks display in your microwave.

When you need to reheat or defrost something in the microwave, do not use metal containers; otherwise your microwave might short circuit.

Family

If you are five years old and your older brother is making you Ready Brek Porridge for breakfast, be prepared that instead of milk he might use fabric softener and you might die.

Do not underestimate the ingenuity of a mum. For example, during a war she might come up with a way to make banana sandwiches with boiled parsnips doused in banana essence.

Do not add sugar when cooking for babies and kids; it brings unnecessary calories and encourages a sweet tooth.

Do not allow babies close to the oven.

Do not allow your husband to bury your failed Christmas Pudding in the garden; otherwise this will become a family story passed down the generations, and they will doubt your cooking prowess until the day you die.

Do not feed your children Pasta Puttanesca. Black olives, capers, and anchovies are not a good children combination.

Do not forget to move domestic arguments out of the kitchen during food preparation. Or else saucepans banged against the kitchen top will change shape and the lid will never fit properly again.

Do not forget to sit as a family around a table when you eat because food is good for bringing people together.

Do not leave a pan on to boil for more than seven hours, as you will then need to replace every single item in your house made of cloth or material. Your wife will refer to this as smoke damage and insist that it has put a strain on your relationship.

Do not let your wife cook.

Do not put pasta in the pot before it boils or your cousin will go mental and tell you that it is ruined.

Do not start a conversation about cooking with the entire family present at the same time!

Do not tell your wife she is doing it wrong.

Do not try copying your mom. Certain dishes never taste as good as she can do them.

How not to cook in an Italian family: Never use curly parsley, never salt your food before tasting it, and never put Parmesan cheese on any pasta dish that has fish in it.

If, as a child, you love the mystery of the kitchen cabinets and have a desire to experiment: Do not empty a whole tub of ground cloves into a saucepan when trying to figure out how to make a curry. Do not try to make baked potatoes by turning the oven up to 125°F with no concept of how hot that is. After four hours they will still be raw.

Do not play the game Poisons with your brother and sister, creating foul-smelling, strange-colored concoctions from anything and everything you find in the kitchen cabinets. Especially enticing are the ingredients none of you knows what to do with—the gelatin leaves, the star anise, the semolina, sliced pieces of Jerusalem artichokes (weird, rubbery, slimy things that smell of potato), the little glass bottles of food colorings and flavorings and packets of unknown herbs and spices.

If for Father's Day you decided to make a jar of "Daddy's Sauce," consisting of several Oxo cubes, confectioners' sugar, allspice, mace, cloves, mixed herbs, and silver decorative balls in addition to a large amount of bicarbonate of soda, bottled in a large Nescafé jar, labeled, and presented it to your father, be prepared that while delighted with the gift, he might gradually pour it down the sink over the next few months, all the while exclaiming that he enjoyed it with his supper after you had gone to bed.

If you and your little sister love the idea of Angel Delight but cannot find the sweet dessert packet in your cupboard, do not try to make up the ingredients yourselves. Confectioners' sugar, pink and yellow food coloring, and milk does not add up to a flavor or color you would want to see, or try, again.

If your mom is trying to make some bread and after about two hours in the oven she pulls out two containers filled with a substance which clings to the sides and bottom like something in a drained pond, it might be that the yeast has not risen, but sunk. If your mom then puts the two pans on the radiator to try to bring the yeast to life but after a day she throws the substance in the garden for the wildlife to choke on, she might never try making bread again. In fact it might provoke the imminent death of your mom's desire to cook for her family and thus destroy the one unifying family experience that you might ever have had.

Never try to cook with little children unless you have all your ingredients and equipment ready. They get impatient and start throwing things around. Put a big shower curtain on the floor under where they are working to catch any falling eggs, etc.

When baking Burnt Butter Biscuits with your eighty-three-year-old grandmother, avoid using glass mixing bowls. There is every chance that she will reach to get the golden syrup out of the cupboard and knock over a bottle of tomato sauce, which will fall out of the cupboard, land upon, and smash the mixing bowl. Gravity will then take hold, propelling the broken mixing bowl from the table directly onto your foot. You will sever your tibialis anterior. You will spend two months in a plaster cast. You may never wear high heels or kick a football again. And it all could have been avoided if the mixing bowl had been made of metal.

When baking, do not let a child decide how much of an ingredient to put in a recipe. They usually do not use measuring cups, particularly when adding sugar or chocolate chips.

When baking with a three-year-old, do not think that with their helpful contribution you will have an edible outcome. It is easiest if you just cut out the middleman and save energy—give them a bowl of sugar to eat and go and buy yourself some doughnuts.

When teaching your children to be ethical consumers, do not enjoy certain products yourself, or you may find a notice about the ethics of consuming on your morning Nescafé, taped to the coffee bottle.

When you are told that your mom will no longer cook for you because you have become a vegetarian and she does not want to be cooking an additional menu, take some cooking lessons. Otherwise you may spend a year making inedible glop and baking bread that can be used as a weapon.

Do not add eggs to bread dough. If your husband, who has never cooked before, decides he wants to bake bread, he will get all the ingredients out, ready with the recipe. You will ask him if he would like help but he will insist you leave the kitchen and not disturb him. He will start mixing the ingredients, and, when it comes to kneading the dough, he will think that he can add a couple of eggs. When trying to get the mixture out of the bowl, he will not be able to. It will be so sticky that he will just keep getting covered in dough. Soon it will be all over him and he will be up to his elbows. You will hear his struggles and come to see him, and you will have fits of laughter. If you then assist him, you too will end up covered—it will be like super glue! You will end up having to throw the whole lot away.

When children are baking a cake and the recipe calls for two tablespoons of rum, do not assume that they will know the difference when you replace it with rum extract—they will still get totally smashed.

When you have accidentally added dishwashing liquid to your salad instead of oil, do not attempt to wash it out and serve it to your children. They will be able to tell the difference. Even the teenagers.

When your partner, who has very little experience in the kitchen, nervously yet excitedly hopes to cook a nice meal for you, and you are a control freak ex-cook who is overbearing, do not shout at the way she chops carrots, making her cry into the tomato sauce. You will feel bad and go away in shame, knowing you have been hurtful. When she serves the pasta and you taste it, all you will think of is her tears. You will taste them in the sauce. Out of frustration, do not tell her it is disgusting and throw it away. Just tell her how much you appreciate her, no matter what her food tastes like.

Fires

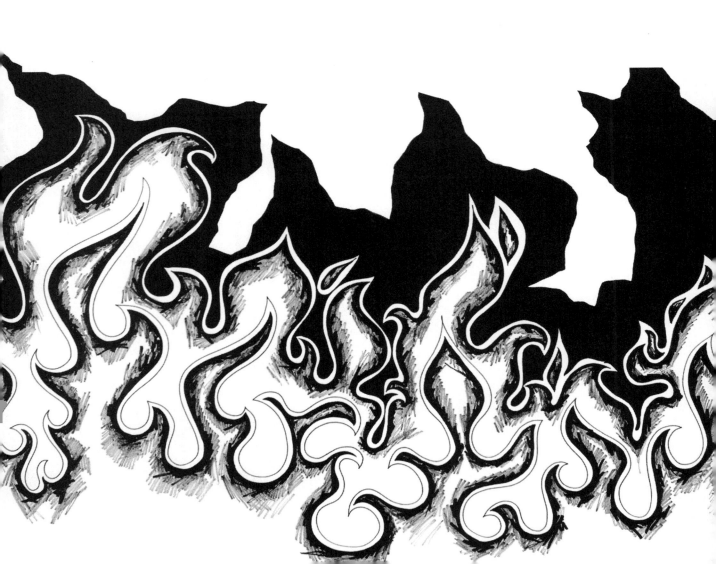

Do not barbeque in a nylon negligee for fear of sparks.

If you are wearing a bathrobe and you are taking something out of the oven, make sure that your sleeves do not catch fire.

When your frying pan catches fire, do not try to put it out with water—you could end up burning your whole kitchen down.

Never make a flambé if you have long hair and bushy eyebrows, especially if you are someone who likes to get really near the pan to smell how things are cooking.

If you want to cook Scaloppini al Brandy, do not add too much brandy when doing the flambé if you do not want to be bald or throw away the hood of the oven.

Do not try to take a glowing pot off the flame. Just turn off the flame!

Be very careful when flambéing. A slippery piece of sugared fruit can easily fall into the burning methylated spirits, splashing the spirits onto the tablecloth and spreading the flame. Should this occur, ignore the temptation to stub out the flames with paper napkins.

When making a flambé, before you set fire to anything, it is a very good idea to make sure that you do not have your face over the frying pan—that is, if you want to keep your eyebrows, eyelashes, and hair intact.

When steaming clams on the stovetop, do not do so in a covered stockpot full of white wine. When you lift the lid to check on the clams the wine vapors will drip from the lid onto the stove flame and it will catch on fire. This will trail up to the pot causing a burst of flames, which will set your hair on fire, flash-toast your face, and give your skin a painful, sunburnlike sensation—but without the sunny glow.

When trying to make Welsh Rarebit, if the pan of boiling oil catches fire, do not mistakenly run it under the sink. The curtains will catch fire, and if you open the window it will be like a fan to the flame.

Do not let oil or butter heat up too much. If it catches on fire, do not use water to put it out.

Do not put plastic wrap next to an electric cooker. Melts, sticks, stinks.

Do not put water on oil fires.

Never leave the kitchen when something is on the stove or everything will burn. You do not want your house to catch on fire!

Never leave oven gloves near a burner. The same can be said for wooden spoons.

Do not attempt to microwave leftover pizza still wrapped in aluminum foil. This is a sure way to start a lovely kitchen fire—unless, of course, that is your intention.

Do not boil Crisco. Do not go fishing and catch so many fish that you do not know how to cook them all. Do not decide to use one of those old-fashioned cloth baby diaper heaters (three-gallon pots that dry the diapers) and melt two mugs of Crisco in the heater. Do not crank up the heat and wait for the Crisco to boil. White flames will start shooting up from the heater, smoke will be everywhere. Neighbors will come out and alarms will go off. You will start with big fish and end up with tiny, shriveled little fish.

If your pan catches fire, DO NOT throw water into it! Just cover the pan with a lid, in order to suffocate the flames.

Do not hire a mouthy sixteen-year-old to deep-fry tofu, with no supervision, at your Indonesian take-out. While he is busy gloating to his customers, the oil will overheat and ignite.

Do not leave the house and attend a concert while a chicken is simmering on your stove. A seven hour chicken can turn out to be delicious. But the likelihood that after you return you will find a couple of firemen in your kitchen is much higher. So if you want to try the slow cooking method, turn on the radio for the concert and stick to your kitchen.

Do not microwave metal objects.

Do not microwave one leaf of kale on high for five minutes in order to experiment. It will catch fire, break the microwave's glass rotating plate, scorch the inside of the microwave permanently, and fill the kitchen with smoke.

Do not put a polyester blanket in the hot oven even if you want the pizza dough to rise during a cold day.

Do not put water on burning oil; it will light your knish on fire.

Do not start grilling black pudding at 3 a.m. on January the first after a night of New Year's celebrations and then fall asleep. You may wake not to a black pudding roll but a black house a couple of hours later.

Do not throw water on a pan filled with olive oil on an electric stove.

If by unfortunate chance your cooking catches fire, do not immediately call the fire brigade. Simply put the lid on your saucepan and wait for the flames to naturally dissipate. Obviously, unless your meals involve smoky flavors, dispose of your pan.

If your father puts an aluminum pot into the microwave, it will create a storm followed by a sinister fog, and you will have to throw away the microwave!

Never cook with a towel on your arm.

Never pour water into hot oil.

Take care when igniting apple brandy. It will produce three-foot-high flames.

Unless the desired effect is to fill the room with smoke, do not heat mince pies in a microwave oven. For that matter, any pastry dough and butter combination will make a very cool flaming effect inside the microwave oven.

When baking a rich and fruity Guinness Cake for its allocated two hours, do not forget to check the oven's settings. Make sure the setting is on "oven" rather than "grill"—this will save you from having to evacuate the hotel.

When boiling water in a plastic electric kettle, be sure not to place the kettle on a electric or gas stovetop, as this will burn the base of the kettle and fill the house with toxic gases and possibly burn the house down. When using a plastic electric kettle be sure to use the provided electric power cord, a domestic power socket, and a safe bench or table.

When cooking with a few pots on the go, do not lose concentration and let your oven glove catch fire, unless life-threatening situations make you hungry.

When heating a croissant in the microwave, if you have left it in too long and it has gone hard, do not assume that another three minutes will sort it out. It will not, and the fire brigade prefers toast anyway.

When making Spanakopita, go light on the butter brushed onto the layers of phyllo dough. Too much butter may make it catch on fire—starting a fire in the oven and flames licking up the walls of your girlfriend's kitchen. Also, do not try to put it out with a fire extinguisher, peel off the gross chemical layers, and then try to serve it at a potluck. No one will be impressed.

When standing over the stove, take care to remove one's hair from the vicinity of the gas burner. The smell of singed hair lingers in a room and will disrupt both the flavors of the food and the performance of calm.

When using the barbeque, use proper lighters. Do not try to make it more fun with gasoline or any other type of fuel, as this may cause sudden spurts and maybe a fire.

When your roommate does not eat that healthy, does not cook that often, or whenever he does cook, it is a disaster—do not eventually get him into eating baked potatoes, an easy and relatively healthy alternative to the usual mush he lived on. He will forget about the oven and when you get home the fire brigade will be there waiting. The whole apartment will stink of smoke and then you will see it—a tiny black coal on the table, the baked potato! Do not live with roommates who cannot cook!

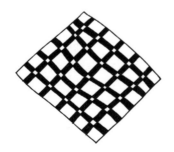

Fish

Do not stir-fry canned tuna fish. Interestingly enough, it does not stir-fry well.

It is not necessary to boil everything for twenty minutes—for example, oysters.

When cooking fish fillets, do not leave them on the stove for too long; they will overcook. Just sear them on high heat and finish in the oven at 400°F for five minutes.

Do not assume that just because you really love fish, you will still love it after buying a whole fresh mackerel. After gutting and deboning it, you may find that you cannot even stand the thought of eating it, and that even the smell turns your stomach.

Do not forget to use aluminum foil to wrap food and prevent it from overcooking on the barbeque.

And when cooking fish, unless you are a pro, do not forget to wrap it in foil or your fish will be dry and destroyed over the grill.

Do not fry fish in a cast-iron pan, because the taste gets absorbed in the iron and will make your next meal taste like seafood.

If holding a squid's eyes firmly while you cut off the tentacles just beneath them disgusts you, you can hold onto the tentacles instead while you cut off the head, but since they are very slippery, the chances of cutting your fingers increase radically.

If you are making crab cakes, do not add too many capers. They are too salty and they will overpower your dish, hiding all the other ingredients.

If you make stuffed squid, do not forget some colorful side dish, or it will look like a pale dolphin's penis.

Putting a lobster in a pot head first might be a problem if the lobster holds on to the edge of the pot with the claws, but no matter how difficult this seems do not try to put the tail in first with the claws pointing at you.

When baking a Backhendl or fried fish in fat, do not use the wrong temperature. When too low, the meat or fish will soak up the fat like a sponge. When too hot, the outside will burn.

When cooking a meal, do not mix fish and meat. When meat has the taste of fish, it is simply unpleasant!

When cooking a whole fish, such as butterfish, be sure to remove the scales before smearing with olive oil and throwing in the lime, chile, and coriander. The scales, when baked, have the texture and appearance of unwashed fingernails and are likely to be inedible for even the politest of your guests.

When cooking crustaceans, make sure to remove their long, black intestinal tract; do not just eat it, or you will eat shit for many years before you realize what it actually is.

When cooking octopus, do not boil it. It will make it chewy and hard. Bring water to a boil and then submerge your octopus three times, pausing between dips. This will cook the fish but not overcook it. You know it is ready when it becomes pinkish or changes color.

When cooking sand crabs, do not forget to throw them in boiling water for a few seconds first, just so that they can pee. Crabs do this as a defense mechanism because they are alive. After they pee, remove them from that water and cook them in clean water or broth or in any other way you want.

When grilling Surf 'n Turf, do not cook the fish before the meat. Otherwise your meat will taste like fish. It will be Surf 'n Surf.

When you buy fish, make sure to keep it refrigerated properly. Take it out of the fridge just before you cook it—not before.

Do not mix fish and cheese together. It is a horrible thing.

Fruit

Do not cut fruit for a fruit salad on the same wooden cutting board that you used for garlic and onion. The final result is revolting.

Do not assume that fruit is sweet enough when making a pie. Forget the sugar in a cherry pie, and it will be unbearably sour.

Do not boil avocado. Tastes like soap.

Do not chop mango on the same board that you have just used to chop onion; the result will be disgusting.

Do not combine melon with other ingredients or you will get indigestion.

Do not cut fruit for your Müesli on the same board as you cut onions or garlic.

Do not drink bottled juice, because it is acidic.

Do not drink water after eating fruits that contain pits, such as grapes, apricots, prunes, and peaches. If you do so, you will be bloated and have stomach problems, especially in the summer.

Do not eat anything for at least a half hour after eating fruit.

Do not forget to put a freshly cut pineapple in salt water. It helps to neutralize the sourness and keeps it fresh longer.

Do not try adding kiwi fruit to cream or yogurt cakes. It turns bitter when combined with any dairy products.

Do not use a metal rasp for rasping apples. Always use a special glass rasp. The metal ions bind to the acid, and the apple loses its taste. It will also be less healthy.

Do not use mango chutney as a sweetener and do not put it in bean paste.

If you are making a fruit salad, do not prepare it too long before serving, especially if you are adding bananas or apples. Or they will go brown or black, and your salad will look bad. Another option is to slice the fruits and squeeze a lemon or an orange over them. The juice will make your salad tastier and the citric acid will prevent your fruits from going brown.

If you make fruit salad and add kiwi, do not keep the kiwi in there for too long or the whole salad will taste bitter.

If you pick your own blackberries and are preparing a blackberry smoothie, do not wash them before dropping them in the blender. If you add them unwashed, you will hopefully taste those wonderful blackberry flower pollen flavors.

If you refrigerate bananas they will turn black! But the fruit still tastes good.

When cutting apples for use in cake or pies, do not leave them for more than two minutes, as this causes discoloration. Soak the cut-up apples in cider to retain their natural color and taste.

When making apple chutney, do not let it cook for too long or the apples will get mushy and lose their sweetness. Also, if you have a choice of vinegars, white wine vinegar is maybe not the best for this.

You must not drink fresh orange juice right away after having pressed it or you will lose the vitamins. Wait three minutes.

Do not mix your sweet with your savories. Avoid raisins in curry and pineapple on pizza.

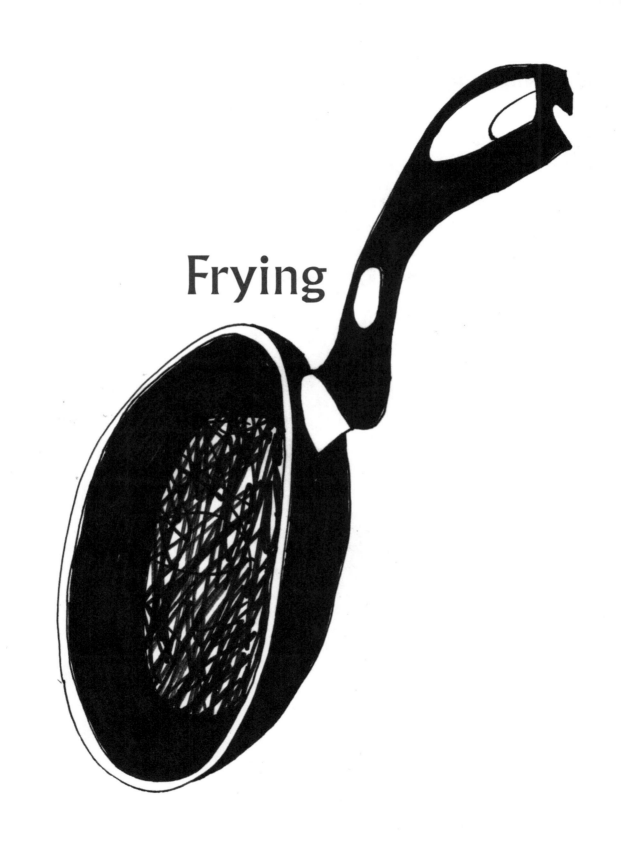

Frying

ALWAYS preheat your pot, pan, or oven if you are going to bake, sauté, broil, fry, or sear. Do not start counting your cooking time if the thing you are putting your food on or in is not hot. Especially if you are deep-frying something.

If the oil is not hot, your food will absorb a lot of oil and will not cook. You will end up with greasy and undercooked meat or vegetables.

Any dish will taste better if you do not burn the oil. Put two toothpicks in the oil to avoid this.

Do not forget to serve lemon with fried foods: The acidity helps with digestion.

Do not fry chips while wearing shorts.

Do not fry frogs.

Do not fry your plantain to stones in old or used oil. They will not have the golden color or crunchy texture you want.

Do not just use butter when you cook. Add some olive oil too so the butter does not burn and you keep the flavor.

Do not use the same oil to fry something more than twice.

If you are frying something, do not let water come close to the oil. It will burst automatically, and boiling oil will jump to your face.

For crispier French Fries, slice them and keep them in a bowl with ice and cold water before frying, but do not forget to shake them before you throw them in the fryer.

If you do not want your kitchen to be transformed into a warehouse of pyrotechnic toys, remember to use a cloth to thoroughly dry and wring out the liquid from calamari before frying the calamari in hot oil.

Unless you are wearing a frying helmet, remember that water and hot oil is a danger zone. When deep-frying, it is very important not to forget to put things in the hot oil dry and gently. If you fry potatoes, let them drain well and salt them lightly—that will take the water away nicely. If you are frying something more watery, like sweet peppers, batter them first in a light runny batter made of water and flour. For almost everything else, use plain flour or corn flour.

When frying vegetables, do not put the veggies in at the same time as the oil.

When deep-frying food in about an inch of very hot oil, be very aware of where your skillet's handle is in relation to your elbow, especially if your small dog is standing directly underfoot. If you do not, said dog may live the rest of its life with a patch of skin on its back from which no hair will ever grow again.

When frying calamari that has been frozen, do not stand too close to the frying pan, because frozen calamari retains a lot of water and the oil will pop and explode in your face, leaving you to walk around with a face full of blisters.

When you bread fish to fry, first dip it in the flour and then the egg, not the other way round.

Gadgets

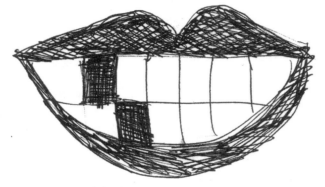

It's perfect

An instant thermometer reads temperatures almost instantly. DO NOT insert it in the roast and put it in the oven unless you like a garnish of melted plastic.

As a general note, do not use fancy machines, like a pit extractor or an electric carrot grater. Your food will not necessarily turn out any better!

Chickpeas can be cooked quickly and easily in a pressure cooker, but before closing it you have to remember to put water in.

Do not attempt to stop the juicer with a ten-inch kitchen knife, as the turning action of the juicer will jettison the knife at any uncertain angle at a high velocity.

Do not blend Nettle Soup with one of those Magic Wand stick blenders while wearing a white sweater.

Do not mash your potatoes with a stick blender; it will eliminate the lumps but will also turn the potatoes into a paste, because the blender activates the starch of your potatoes. The best thing about mashed potatoes is that they are mashed, not blended. A few pieces and lumps are good.

Do not put wheatgrass in your Champion juicer; it will clog everything up. You need a separate juicer designed to process grasses.

Do not try to create a meringue without an electric mixer. Using a whisk to make meringue takes a long time, and your arm will start to fall off.

Do not try to open a pressure cooker before all the steam has escaped. You need to be patient and wait for the little knob to go down.

A pressure cooker is invaluable for making tasty soup stock and stews out of bones and cheaper cuts of meat, but do not, whatever you do, leave it unattended, unless you have checked your insurance and plan to redecorate the house anyway.

If the recipe says "fold in gently," do not use an electric beater.

If you are the lucky owner of an Aga or Rayburn cast-iron oven, do not forget about what you put inside, because there are no lights or see-through glass to see what is cooking.

If you use an oven such as a Rayburn or an Aga, do not forget that no smells escape from the cast-iron doors. Whole chickens have been discovered.

Never make Hollandaise Sauce directly on heat; put it in a bain-marie or in a Thermomix.

Truffle oil is very potent. "Use sparingly" does not mean teaspoons, it means drops.

When making a Key Lime Pie, where the recipe calls for lime zest and you do not own a zester, do not assume chopping the peel will work. Invest in a zester or at least work very, very hard at chopping the peel finely. Cooked chunky pieces of lime peel are not tasty.

When using a pressure cooker, do not remove the valve.

When whipping cream with an electric beater, it will turn to butter. Do not overbeat anything.

When you get an ice cream maker, assemble it properly. The paddle that sits in the middle of the churning bowl is supposed to stay still to fluff air into the ice cream. Do not allow the paddle to turn. If you do, your ice cream does not freeze or fluff properly and becomes a dense, pastelike substance that makes you sick when you eat it because it is so rich.

When you make Icelandic Pancakes, use a special pancake pan. Never, ever wash it; just wipe it with a kitchen towel. Otherwise you will be cursed.

You do not need lots of fancy kitchen tools to clutter up your cupboards, but do invest in a decent knife and do not forget to sharpen it regularly. Chopping vegetables and preparing ingredients will be so much less time-consuming and easier. You are also more likely to cut yourself with a blunt knife.

Garlic

Pour a few drops of olive oil in your hands before you cut, chop, or slice onions and garlic, to prevent odor from staying on your hands—but do not use too much, or it will be dangerous.

When flavoring heated oil with garlic, do not let the garlic brown or the whole meal you are about to prepare will get bitter.

Always remember that a clove of garlic is only a very small proportion of a bulb of garlic. Five bulbs of garlic in a Spaghetti Bolognese is a very garlicky ragu indeed.

Avoid storing onions and potatoes in close proximity. Onions produce gases that can cause potatoes to sprout.

Do not ever put garlic in at the beginning of cooking a dish; add it at the end, when it gives out far more flavor.

Do not forget that garlic and onions will burn faster if put in the pan after the oil is already hot.

Do not forget that the good part about garlic is the outside, not the inside. This is why in fine cuisine garlic is crushed with a knife. If you do not remove the green root from inside, your dish will taste bitter.

Do not forget that the base of the dish, such as fried onion and celery, is the most important.

Do not fry onions and garlic together in a copper or iron pot, or they will turn bright green. This is caused by a chemical reaction between the natural sulphurous compounds that the bulbs make and heavy metals usually found in the onions or garlic depending on their soil conditions. The heavy metals added to the soil are typically copper, zinc, iron, and manganese. While this is not toxic or dangerous, do not continue cooking with the green onions. Everyone will be horrified.

Do not fry your onions or your garlic for too long, or they will turn bitter and inedible!

Do not stand directly above the onions you are cutting.

Do not fry onions quickly. They are best and more tasty if left for fifteen minutes to cook slowly.

If you are chopping a fresh onion for a recipe, and your eyes start to burn and water, do not use eye drops to make your eyes feel better! Your eyes will feel like they are on fire! To stop the tears, keep the onion in the fridge beforehand, or just walk away from the onion for a while until your eyes stop watering and the vapors from the onion disperse.

If you do not want your sliced fruit to taste like garlic, reserve a separate cutting board to slice garlic.

Never add too much garlic to Pesto Sauce. One piece is enough.

When making Pesto, do not throw the entire clove of garlic into the mixer. If it is ripe enough, the thick and green center will make the sauce spicy, bitter, and impossible to digest.

Never chop onions; cut them. Cutting them keeps the cells intact, lessens the emission of the gas that makes you tear, and keeps them from getting bitter.

Never, ever use garlic that comes out of a spray can! And especially not when you are making a fresh garden salad.

Never lightly fry onions with Coke.

Never use a garlic press; it makes the garlic bitter. If you want it crushed, crush it with a knife.

Never, ever use garlic if you are cooking for the British.

To get rid of the smell of garlic on your hands, do not rub them under a running tap—you are really rubbing in the smell. Just let the water run over your hands.

When adding fresh garlic to hummus, do not just put a few finely chopped cloves into the mix, as your guests will taste garlic in their mouths for the whole day. Instead, put the finely chopped garlic together with the oil, lemon, and salt for a half hour and it will not taste so strong.

When making an onion pie, do not use too many ingredients. Keep it simple. For example, if you are making the pie with onions and cheese, do not add tomatoes. It will just get uselessly heavy.

When sautéing onions, make sure you sauté them separately from other ingredients until they are translucent in order to get rid of the bitter taste or you will realize why children say they hate onions.

When storing fresh, peeled garlic, do not just leave it out. This will reduce its nutritional properties.

When you are cooking with garlic, never forget to cut it first in half and take the green germ out. The germ gives the whole dish a bitter taste.

When you slice onions, never forget to turn your eyes away from the cutting board. However, if you do want to look into the eyes of the enemy, put some sunglasses on. This adds a trendy touch to the ambiance of your kitchen and also protects the onions from your flowing tears.

While chopping an onion, do not cut off the ends along with the skin or the layers of the onion will fall apart when you cut it in half. Keep and hold on to the roots instead while cutting the onion.

Do not burn garlic or it will become bitter.

Do not throw whole garlic cloves and bell peppers into your pasta sauces at random.

Gender

Do not check out the benefits to your arms when whisking meringue because someone will notice and you will be teased forever.

Do not hang around pregnant women with bizarre cravings.

Do not wear your wife's new dress while cooking Spaghetti Sauce.

In classic feminine multitasking style, do not cook while also loading the washing machine or applying sealant to tiles. This can lead to severe confusion with disastrous results. Do not lick your fingers, assuming it is yogurt. You will only discover that it is, in fact, concentrated laundry detergent, which on consumption of water produces a river of bubbles from the mouth.

In order not to cook it is advisable to be born male in a family where traditional gender roles are assiduously maintained. Should you have the misfortune to be born female, it is a relief that contemporary Western society is able to provide you with an inexhaustible range of instant products that do not require any understanding of the use of knives or the application of heat. In fact it could be said that current circumstances have never been more favorable for the demise of cooking, whether in fact you are male or female!

When not cooking because of subconscious feminism, avoid anorexia. If dependent on scholarship to study art in Paris, when subject to subconscious feminism, do not go to restaurants to avoid cooking. When cooking becomes as expensive as eating in restaurants, consider anorexia.

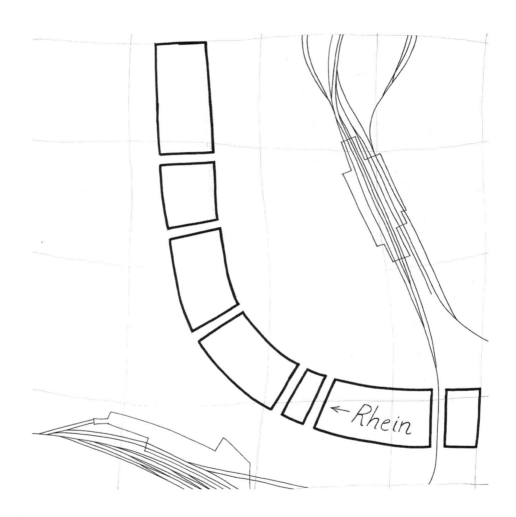

Rhein

Germany

Spaetzle are not to be left in the water after being cooked. Do not ask why. Do not try this. It is disgusting.

Do not believe that readymade potato dumplings have anything in common with the real handmade dish called Thuringian Dumplings, even if you are trying to fake it by using readymade dough and putting the toasted bread inside the dumpling to add the handmade look. Do not believe that your mother-in-law, especially if she is from Thuringia, will not be able to see the difference the very moment the dumplings arrive at the dinner table.

Do not forget that Springerle, Swabian cookies, can be baked only in the kitchens of Swabian aunts. It is not your fault if it does not work anywhere else.

Do not put the spaetzle in the water before the water is fully boiling.

Do not save your energy when stirring pudding and gelatin for Black Forest Gâteau. If not well stirred, the granules will spoil the fun.

If you try to bake gluten-free Swabian Pfitzauf, do not be disappointed if the dough does not rise the slightest bit.

For Königsberger Klopse, do not use the regular version of mixed pork and beef but use ground veal instead. Do not add salt but finely sliced anchovies instead. For the sauce, prepare a roux by melting butter and stirring in flour. When the mix turns golden, do not just add pure water but stock, along with some vinegar and sugar to reach the typical sweet and sour taste that goes with the capers.

When making spaetzle, do not forget to add salt to the egg mass. Do not put the egg mass in the refrigerator before cooking the dish. You want to do the opposite! Place the egg mass in a warm area for five minutes—this will give the spaetzle a nice gold color.

If you are going to make the traditional Frankfurter Grüne Soße (Frankfurt Green Sauce), which is a recipe created by Goethe's mother, do not leave the ready-to-cook package of seven fresh herbs—borage, parsley, burnet, cress, sorrel, chervil, and chives—longer than two days in the refrigerator. If you wait any longer than this, you may possibly be able to rescue some parsley and chives for your scrambled eggs.

When preparing a Labskaus, do not try to substitute for the corned beef. Neither canned beef nor some leftovers from the previous dinner will do.

When you are making a Wiener Schnitzel, do not cook it in cold fat.

Tafelspitz should not be cooked with spices, despite what most people think and say. The meat and spices do not marry well together.

When preparing Poached Carp, a classic German Christmas dish, do not forget to water the fish for a couple of hours before preparation. Otherwise it will taste moldy and your guest will despairingly ask for cheese sandwiches instead.

When using the popular Italian coffee maker for caffè espresso, do not forget to put water into the percolator. First, no coffee will be brewed. And second, the coffee powder will freeze together with the gasket, stinking like hell. Any rescue attempts are likely to end with burned fingers. If you remember to add the water to the percolator but forget to insert the strainer between the coffee powder and the upper part of the metal pot, step back and search for cover. The explosion will leave coffee stains all over your kitchen wall that will shine through even three layers of new white paint.

When preparing an entire goose or duck, always check the inside before stuffing it. German butchers tend to put the innards in a plastic sack in there. If not removed, the melted plastic will ruin the whole roast.

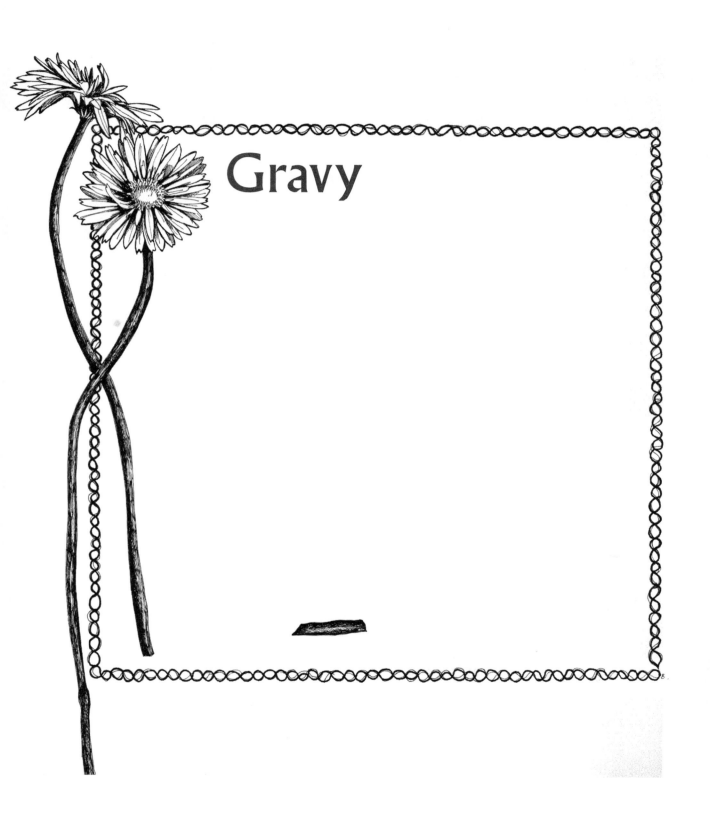

Gravy

Do not put the flour directly into the gravy even if you are in a hurry. Lumps.

Do not add cornstarch directly to the sauce; mix it with water first.

Do not add mustard to a sauce until the end, or it will have a weird taste.

Do not change too often the sense of rotation when stirring sauces or creams.

Do not let Tomato Sauce come to a full boil or it will taste bitter.

Do not make sauces with tons of cream. It is passé and difficult to digest. A little cream is okay to tone down a sauce, but cream itself should not be the base for a sauce. You need to work hard on a sauce with stocks and other ingredients and add just a little cream at the end to make it smooth.

Do not rely on cream for the gravy. It is a cheap trick. The gourmet chef uses a shredded onion, wine, and a little tomato pulp. Let this boil down in the pan.

For the Béchamel Sauce, do not add the flour after the milk boils; this will never allow the flour to dissolve, and your guests will find little dry treasures in it.

Do not thicken your boiling hot stews, gravies, and sauces by adding flour or starch without first dissolving it in another cooler liquid. Unless, of course, you want dumplings that are not good.

Do not use clarified butter when cooking, especially when making Hollandaise Sauce. You want to use real butter.

If you are making a tomato sauce from scratch for your pasta, the tomatoes may be a bit acidic. If you do not add sugar while you are cooking them in order to reduce their acidity, they will give you heartburn.

If you are preparing a tasty tomato sauce and you forget the tomato concentrate, do not worry. You will most certainly have some ketchup in the fridge, and your guests will never know the difference.

Never take your eyes off a cooking Béchamel or it will rebel and go all rubbery.

To give shine to your sauce, do not forget to add, at the end of cooking, one or two spoons of cornstarch diluted in a bit of cold water. Boil it for a few minutes until it gets the right texture. The result will be much like the sauces in a Chinese restaurant. It is indeed one of their secrets!

When making Béchamel Sauce, do not mix the flour with hot milk because it will become very lumpy. Use cold water instead.

When using cornstarch to thicken a sauce, always dissolve it in cold liquid first and then add it to the pot slowly. If you do not, it is difficult to judge when your sauce has thickened to the right consistency, and instead your spoon will end up like the legendary Sword in the Stone.

Herbs

A teaspoon of dried basil is not equivalent to a teaspoon of fresh basil.

Do not throw away the roots and stalks of cilantro or parsley. They can be chopped up and have lots of flavor.

The phrase "small green herbs" is not enough information for a written recipe or a shopping list.

Do not add fresh herbs at the beginning of cooking. They lose their aroma while cooking, so add them only at the end.

Do not boil parsley or basil.

Do not cook parsley if you do not want to poison your friends. Only serve parsley raw.

Do not use preground herbs. They do not have real flavor. Instead, have a shrub of rosemary, thyme, sage, and parsley on your windowsill. But do not try this with basil. Basil hardly survives.

Do not use basil seeds in place of fresh basil.

For any kind of dish, do not add herbs early on in the cooking process. They will just burn and be flavorless. Add your herbs at the very last second to retain their flavor. This particularly applies to when making a nice broth.

If you make Bolognese with ground pork from a recipe you picked up in error and the result is yucky, greasy, and inedible, do not think that adding chiles or herbs will make it taste any better. If you convert it into Lasagna it will taste even worse.

Never put only onions in the tomato sauce. Always use garlic and onion together. Do not add one without the other.

Hosting

POEM:

Hello Beautiful —
it's time to go
don't forget what
you brought along
and why you
came in the
first place.

Do not explain too much what is in your dish. Let them have a bite. If they like it, talk about it. If not, talk about it too.

If you are using olives in a recipe, do not use olives with pits. If you do, please make sure to let your guests know about it; otherwise someone might lose a tooth.

Crazy dishes may not be as exciting to your guests as they are to you, so try to keep your cooking for company fairly nonthreatening. Nonvegans are happy to eat your acorn squash with wild rice, but don't expect them to be as excited about Tofurky as you are.

Do not experiment on guests.

When serving guests, do not fill up their plates too much.

Do not forget to invite guests to your dinner party.

Do not forget to taste your food before offering it to others.

Do not lock yourself inside the kitchen. Make cooking a social event! Let them all take part.

Do not offer second helpings to your dinner guests on a whim, only to find that there really is not enough to go around.

Do not plan a dinner party after recently having your jaw wired shut following surgery. Do not spend hours preparing carrot and orange soup, ratatouille, mashed potatoes, onions in red wine, and mushrooms in brandy. Even if you slave for hours to try to produce nice food with flavor and originality, the reaction from your friends will be one of horror, as the food you prepare will be blended and strained.

Do not pretend that your Gourmet Mo's Readymeals are your own work. The guests will always know.

Do not put dirty dishes in the oven to hide them when friends drop by unexpectedly. Even if you tell your spouse, partner, or roommates that the dishes are in there, they will forget, and so will you. The next time the preheated oven is opened, the food remnants on the plates will have become part of the permanent glaze, and anything plastic will have become modern art.

Do not put pans on the table. It just looks ugly. The same for plastic water bottles.

Do not start setting the table when dinner is ready. If you set the table beforehand, you can take your time cooking and eat while the food is still hot.

Do not try to make lots of new dishes for an important dinner party. You need a lot of practice to make several dishes well at the same time. Concentrate on the main course.

Do not forget to invite or eat with others who enjoy food and cooking just like you.

Eating and cooking is an art, not just something you do. Do not invite people who do not appreciate food and cooking or have poor palates. It will ruin the meal for everyone.

If deciding to cook two lamb chops and your partner says, "What if someone comes? There will be nothing to offer." You may reply, "Who will turn up at this time? That would be rude." Of course, you may find that loads of people will turn up, and you will have to turn the chops into stew.

If something is not cooking fast enough for the dinner call, do not turn up the heat, because the exterior will burn and the interior will remain raw.

If you are having a dinner in a small apartment, do not dare to cook octopus or kidney. It will stink and you will probably lose your appetite.

If you are throwing a dinner party, do not put out too much alcohol before you serve the food you have been cooking all day. Just take out some bottles of wine and save the hard liquor for later. Otherwise your guests will be drunk and not hungry, and they will forget about your fabulous dinner.

If you use old vodka bottles to chill tap water in the refrigerator, be sure to label them properly. If you do not, you might accidentally serve your guests a tall glass of cold vodka.

Never forget to cook a dish at least once before preparing it for a fancy dinner, especially if you are not used to cooking for big parties.

Never test a new recipe on guests. Always cook dishes you are reasonably familiar with, or you risk disaster or delays. Limit yourself to one ambitious dish and keep the rest of the menu easy to assemble and produce. For example, a soup and dessert that you made a day or so beforehand can simply be reheated or served cold. Combine this with one fancy main course that you cook that day or is cooking as your guests arrive, filling your abode with a delicious aroma that greets your guests and whets their collective appetite. Always have a light snack set out to accompany predinner drinks. Remember, the idea is for everyone, including yourself, to have a jolly time, and no one likes it when their host is rushing around in the kitchen the whole night. Careful preparation ensures you are a cool, calm, and collected host. That is the most successful ingredient to entertaining.

The best thing about being the cook is to be able to lick the wooden spoon to see how the food is tasting. But do not do this in front of your guests because it looks really terrible.

When preparing a dinner party do not start to assemble the ingredients at 7 p.m. and then decide to dash off to the shop for a vital missing spice when the guests are arriving at 7:30. Though the food—for example, Stuffed Iraqi Potato Balls—may be delicious, serving it at 11 p.m., when everyone has consumed at least a bottle and a half of wine on empty stomachs, leads only to congealed, barely touched plates. And a riotous evening.

Under NO circumstances are you to serve a dish to your guests without first taste-testing it!

Do not organize a dinner party for midnight. People will be too drunk to appreciate it.

Hot Stuff

Do not prepare spicy food for boring friends who will not appreciate it.

Do not forget that more than three Thai chiles in a dish will deal with your enemies.

Do not dry-fry red chiles without wearing goggles. If goggles are mislaid, keep your distance. Do not look down at the pan, and be ready to stick your head out a window.

Do not lean over a pan to smell the sauce when frying hot chiles; the chile steam will act as tear gas, and you may not be able to feel your lips for a while.

Do not wipe your eyes after preparing sweet or hot peppers. In fact, do not do anything else after preparing peppers until you have washed your hands thoroughly.

A tablespoon of chile powder is not equivalent to a tablespoon of paprika.

Different peoples and cultures have different tastes. Do not forget that the amazing authentic Thai Green Curry recipe you found might cause your guests' mouths to explode.

Do not add sweet chili sauce to every dish you prepare. Please.

Do not buy ground spices for making Indian, Thai, or Mexican dishes. Buy whole spices instead and use a mortar and pestle. Dry-roast whole spices in a thick-bottomed pan over medium heat until they darken slightly and release their aroma. They will also be easier to grind.

Do not chop Scotch bonnet chiles without wearing gloves. No number of buckets of cold water, frozen peas, or milk will ease the throbbing sting.

Do not cook spicy food with the kitchen door open and the kitchen window closed. Your house will smell just too exotic for days or weeks.

Do not inhale fumes from chopped jalapeño peppers.

Do not put your fingers in your mouth after cutting hot peppers.

Do not rub your eyes after cutting jalapeños.

Do not touch eyes or nose after preparing chiles. Men should wash their hands BEFORE going to the toilet.

Do not try to cover up for having added too much chile to the delicious couscous you prepared for about two and a half hours. Your claims will not be heard when your eyes are watering and you cannot stop coughing in between spoonfuls. Rather serve some yogurt with fresh mint on the side.

Do not watch a sad movie while making Chili con Carne; at some point you will rub your eyes and cry even more.

Just because you happen to love very hot and spicy food and lots of garlic does not mean that everyone else does. If you are a fan of these extremes, make sure when preparing a dinner for guests that you scale back drastically; otherwise they might politely decline to eat the food after the first painful bit. You can always add supplemental garlic and hot peppers onto your own plate.

Love habanero peppers? Caution, do not ever mince them with your knife and bare hands. Not only will your hands swell up like two loafs of bread, but you will also be in agony for hours to come. It will penetrate so deep into your skin and eventually find its way to other parts of your body—even down south. Muy caliente!

Never rub your eyes after picking seeds out of a chile pepper.

Never touch your penis after chopping chile peppers without rinsing your hands first. This is especially useful to remember if you go to urinate after chopping chiles.

When cooking Apple Pie, do not let your "It will give it just a little bit of a kick" best friend convince you that your dessert will not be overwhelmingly spicy if you add two entire cayenne peppers into the filling. It will be overwhelmingly spicy. Inedibly spicy.

When making your own Curry Sauce, do not forget that curry powder alone is not enough to enrich the flavor. Add turmeric, coriander, and cumin.

When using chiles in your recipe such as jalapeño, habanero, de árbol, and chipotle, do not forget to cut them in half, open them, and remove the seeds and veins. That is where the heat is. Another way of having the kick, but not getting kicked, is by boiling them first so they lose some of the heat. Never, ever touch your face or eyes while handling chiles.

Do not make love after cutting jalapeños.

Ice Cream

Be careful not to infuse milk with lavender flowers for too long when making Vanilla Lavender Ice Cream, or it will taste more like lavender soap.

Do not attempt to make Papaya Ice Cream. The papaya enzyme content mixed with milk will smell like vomit.

Do not make a fatty ice cream base with whole milk and cream. It will leave a fatty white residue on your tongue.

Do not make ice cream with fresh ginger; it will curdle the milk.

Do not spend three weeks waiting patiently for sorbet to set. If it has not frozen by then, you have probably done something wrong!

Do not try to make Lilac Flower Ice Cream. It will be too bitter.

When baking cookies, even if you are using a lot of butter in your recipe, oil your mold, and then sprinkle some flour onto the surface so that they do not stick. Otherwise you will be eating crumbles instead of cookies. But if you have crumbles, save them and put them over ice cream. Yummy!

When making mashed Wild Strawberry and Brown Sugar Sweet Sauce for your Vanilla Ice Cream, do not leave the small pan on the stove and walk away. When boiling, the sugar turns into caramel very quickly, and when the sauce bubbles up all over on the stove it is not only a mess to clean up, but an absolute heartbreak.

When preparing Russian Tea Ice Cream, an important step is to caramelize the tea. If the liquid does not seem to solidify, try using more sugar. If it is still not working, taste it. There is a certain likelihood that you have used salt instead of sugar. Do not try to mend the mess. Start all over again.

When preparing Saffron Ginger Ice Cream, be aware that saffron is not just for color! It has a very particular flavor, too. Do not use too much or it might make you cringe. Although that shade of yellow really is luscious.

Do not make semifreddo when in a rush. If you do, you will not have the patience to wait for the semifreddo to freeze properly and you will end up just eating cream.

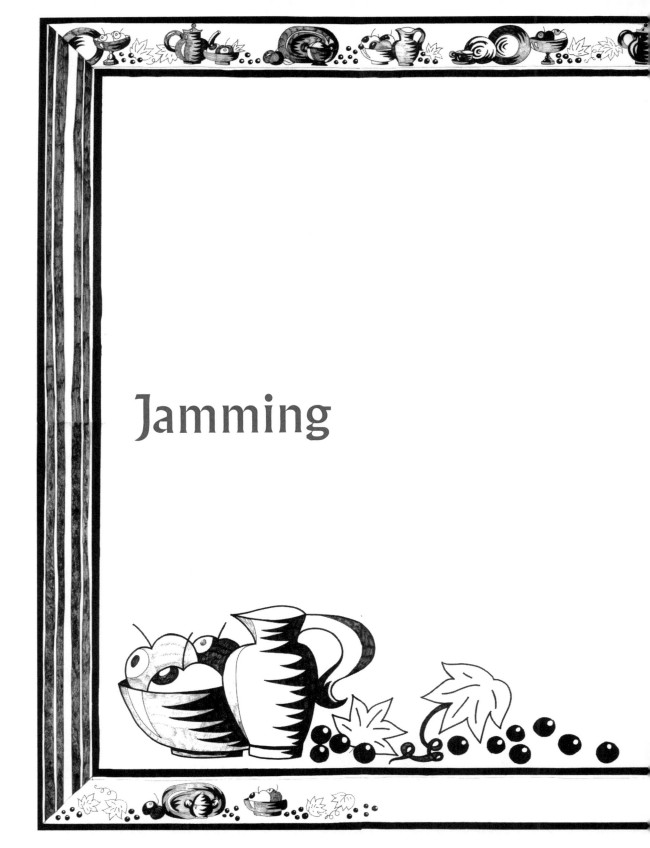

Jamming

When cooking Rhubarb Jam, do not use an aluminum pot, even though the pot will become very nice and clean on the inside. Do not eat the jam!

If you are making Gooseberry Jam, it will set very well because gooseberries have a lot of pectin in them. Do not forget to put a lot of sugar into the jam, because the berries are also very sour.

If you put some of your homemade jam mix in a plate and turn it upside down and it drips, it means that it is not ready yet. Repeat this until it does not drip.

Do not answer the telephone when you are cooking Blackberry Jam.

Do not make jam without any clothes on. When it gets to the hot lava stage, the burns can get really serious.

Do not throw away old jam jars. Instead of paying for the cinema, you could give them your old jam jars and get in for free.

How to (not) make Morello Cherry Jelly:

Take a cherry tree that is full of ripe Morello cherries. Preferably the one in your backyard. Act quickly before the birds get to them; pick lots of berries. Do not fall off ladder.

Do not consult a cookbook. Do not check the Internet for recipes. Proceed from half-memorized recipe for Black Currant Jelly: Same amount water and berries, double amount sugar, bring water and berries to a boil, add sugar, boil some more.

Take out what is left of the berries and pits (squeeze well to retain as much berry juice as possible), fill liquid on sterilized glass jars. Leave in a cold place until tomorrow.

Tomorrow there will be no cherry jelly, only cherry sauce.
Now, bring your sister, who has heard about something called "the jelly test." Pick double amount of cherries together.
Proceed with the same recipe as yesterday, but keep boiling.
Apply the jelly test.
Too early, keep boiling.
Wipe steam off windows.
Apply the jelly test.
Still too early, keep boiling.
Open windows and doors.
Keep boiling.
The jelly test will now seem to indicate that there might be jelly in the making.
Take out berries and pits and proceed like yesterday; you will have cherry jelly for breakfast.

There will be twelve jars of cherry sauce for breakfast.

Do not give up.

Take all the cherry sauce of yesterday and the day before yesterday and chuck it into a very large saucepan.

Send a child out to pick a lot more cherries.

Finely chop four limes.

Add the new berries and sugar, con amore.

Add cognac, con amore. (Don't forget to taste it—it might be old.)

Just let it boil.

Sit in the sun and read the newspaper.

Check on the berries.

Read another newspaper.

Now you take out berries and stones and proceed like normal.

Pray to the Jelly God all evening and most of the night.

The Jelly God will not answer your prayers.

A week later, through an intermediary, he will inform you that, unlike black currants, Morello cherries do not have natural pectin, making them unfit for jelly making without additives.

Kitchen

If you want to use the oven do not forget to turn it on.

Do not heat honey to more than 105°F or it will become toxic.

Do not scrape a nonstick pan with sharp objects or things will stick. Also, if you use a sharp object with a nonstick pan, it can scrape off the coating and then you will be eating nonstick coating with your food.

Never cook with gas! Do not lose faith in the goodness of electricity. It is the safest and most practical way.

Do not cook with electric burners. They are evil! Cook only with gas!

To avoid major disasters when cooking, do not let your skillet handles stick out beyond the stove area.

Always make sure your kitchen appliances are in top-notch working order. If you do not, while making your first Thanksgiving turkey you may open the oven door to baste the turkey and the oven door may fall off!

As a general rule, do not ever use poor-quality produce and products.

Baking soda is a very popular and versatile product. It can be used in many different ways and for many different purposes such as cleaning, whitening teeth, as well as preventing odors in your fridge and on your body. But do not use it for cooking, only for baking.

Clearly label your spice jars, because garlic powder looks a lot like ginger powder and they are easily confused. Ginger goes well with chocolate chip cookies but garlic surely does not.

Do not allow two cooks in the kitchen at the same time. One cook and two assistants is okay, but two cooks is a disaster because everyone has their own way of doing things.

Do not be afraid to blast something that seems off with some heat. It might be dragged back from over the edge.

Do not cook with an electric stove pretending that it is gas.

Do not ever use metal cooking utensils with a Teflon pan; it will scratch the Teflon off and the toxic stuff will fall into your food. In fact, never even use Teflon pans—why risk perfluorooctanoic acid poisoning?

Do not forget that cast iron needs quite a bit of seasoning before it works well.

Do not forget that each ingredient has its function.

Do not forget that if you change the order of the steps in the cooking process, the result will change.

Do not forget to always preheat the oven to the recommended temperature.

Do not freeze soda pop cans.

Do not heat any kind of ingredient above 212°F, or else it just dies.

Do not microwave your food.

Do not overcook anything!

Do not overcook—shorter cooking times preserve more nutrients.

Do not preheat the oven for more than fifteen minutes. After fifteen minutes it is not preheating— it is cooking.

Do not put glass pans or glass cups filled with boiling water under a cold tap or on a cold surface. They will crack.

Do not put plastic covers in the oven.

Do not put raw birds or fish inside a cold oven. Germs and bacteria will spread!

Do not use a plastic spatula when you are frying something, as it will melt.

Do not use a wooden spoon in the blender.

Do not rush, overmix, overcook, overseason, underseason, use a dull knife, waste, be afraid.

Do not cook in a badly lit kitchen—you need to see your food well.

For Christmas dinner, never start to cook if your oven does not work very well.

If a small kitchen requires you to store pans in your oven, do not include any frying pans with rubber or plastic handles. Especially do not put them in the very bottom broiler part. You might not bake for a month or two and forget, and when you finally turn on the oven your house will fill with a faint smell that you will not notice until you begin to get woozy and nauseated. If you accidentally do this, take responsibility for it and do not try to convince your roommate or boyfriend that they did it.

If you cook anything with tomatoes in an iron pot, be sure to take it out of the pot before putting it in the fridge, because if you leave it in there the acid in the tomatoes will dissolve the iron.

If you live in a place where they still use gas canisters and you are cooking an important dinner for twenty, make sure you have enough gas left, or a spare canister.

If you want great results in the kitchen, do not buy your ingredients in a supermarket. Good cooking comes from using good produce.

Do not open the fridge barefoot. If the floor is wet you could get an electric shock.

It is important to remember that you can always add—but you cannot take away.

It may sound a little old-fashioned, but it is much easier to cook with gas instead of electric. Electric cookers can be hard to get used to. It is good to make sure that you are doing everything in your own time when you cook.

Take care, take time, and do not use microwaves—they are just dangerous.

Never be so presumptuous as to think the simplest dish will be ready in five minutes.

Never cook with electricity!

Never put a meal that is still hot into the refrigerator.

Never put hot food in the fridge; it will taste like it went bad, and the steam of the food will overcook whatever you are trying to keep fresh. Wait until it is cold and then refrigerate.

Never try to show off if you are in someone else's kitchen. Their equipment, oven, etc. will be different, and you will end up looking bad!

Never use acrylic aprons in the kitchen.

Never use produce that is not fresh.

This should be obvious, but never try an untried dish on a friend. And doubly so if it is in their kitchen.

Too many cooks spoil the broth! Do not crowd the kitchen with too many people.

Unless it is rotten meat or fish, do not throw anything away. Leftovers can be added to sauces to create new things.

When leaving leftovers in the bottom of the oven after a meal, try not to forget about them before next turning on the oven. This often leads to confused flavors and a lot of smoke.

When oiling a pan with a brush, do not do it when it is hot, otherwise the synthetic hair from the brush will ruin the pan and your dish. Even if your brush is made by Pyrex.

When running water to wash up after cooking, do not pop out to the trash bin without your house keys. The resulting flood will damage your kitchen and potentially cost you an emergency locksmith fee to reopen your door.

Do not forget to turn the oven off when the food is finished cooking.

When working in a field station in Mauritius with an outdoor kitchen, a new oven may be a great source of excitement. When putting a Pineapple Upside-Down Cake to cook in the new oven, however, you may be very disappointed when you take the cake out to find that one side has a very deep cake top, and the other side is bare pineapple.

When you bake a cake for your friend's birthday, do not bake it in a pan that is too small. Make sure you have a pan that is big enough, or the dough will take over your oven.

Lasagna

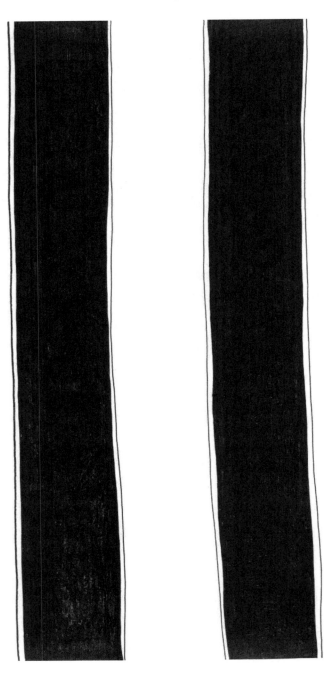

Do not use a pan that is too big to fit in the oven. Make sure that you check the size of whatever pan you are going to use. This will prevent loads of work from being ruined when you find out that you cannot cook that beautiful Lasagna or Casserole.

Do not pour a clotted-up Béchamel Sauce over your Lasagna and think the clots will melt in the oven—they will not.

Do not get distracted when cooking Lasagna and forget the pasta layers.

Do not listen to a vegetarian who wants to cook Vegetable Lasagna using lentils. It will turn out stodgy and tasteless.

When making Lasagna, after layering all the ingredients make sure that you watch it while in the oven so that it does not burn.

Joy   Beauty

Charm

Legs

Do not ignore local custom in regards to seating and serving. If you are invited to a feast in Samoa in the High Chief's ceremonial hut, the seating and serving order will be determined by a strict and ancient code. On one side sits the Ali'I, and next to him are the lesser, or Talking, Chiefs, leading to the other side of the hut, where the women and children reside. If you are seated directly next to the High Chief and all the members of the village sit with legs crossed, but you cannot assume this position for very long, and so finally shift to a semireclining configuration, this will be a fatal error. In a public meeting in the hut, it is taboo to expose one's leg. One of the Talking Chiefs may quickly throw a woven pandanus mat over your legs to make you more presentable.

When, as students, you and your roommate invite a dishy dental student upstairs for dinner, be careful in serving a plateful of sumptuous pasta with barely cooked garlic, onion, herbs, and tomatoes to her. When reaching to pass her the plate, she might cross her legs flamboyantly, thus kicking the plate and its contents sky high.

When trying to cook Coq au Vin, do not buy a leg from some miniature-variety chicken but from a fully formed chicken. Do not marinate the chicken for less than five minutes; otherwise it looks like you are serving a raw rat's leg.

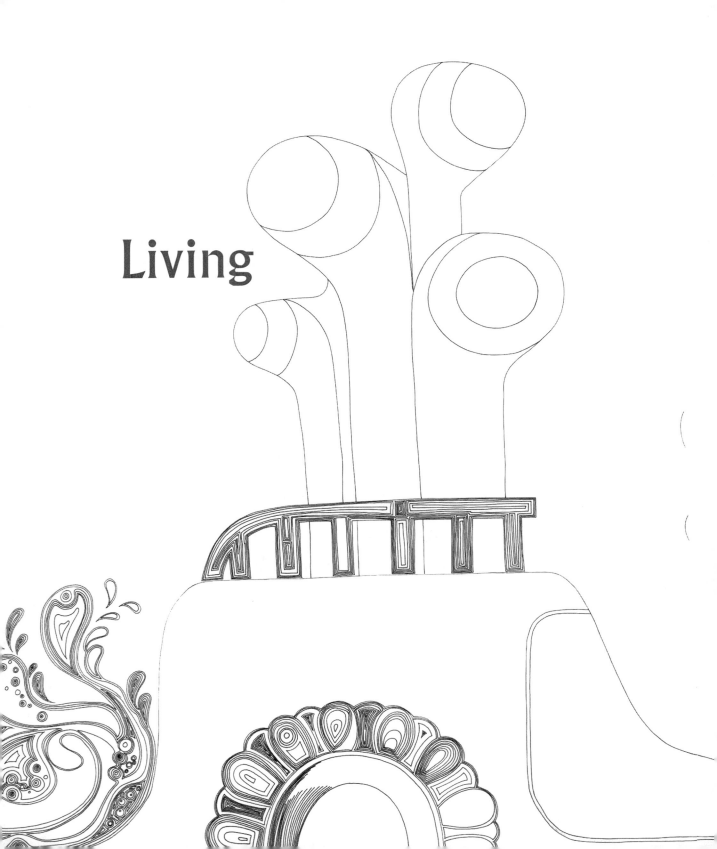

Living

Do not forget that a kitchen is like a pirate boat. You must live with the danger, and the language often changes.

Do not cook when you are in a bad mood.

Do not cut your toenails in the kitchen!

Do not put your finger in the couscous, because it will ruin the result.

Do not eat when you are hungry.

Do not forget love and patience when you are cooking.

Do not forget that cooking is an art—not a science.

When buying fast food, do not order like a kid: fish without the chips, pizza without the cheese, or hamburger without the meat.

Do not hurl a cast-iron Le Creuset casserole dish out the back door of your house onto the patio after having burned the dinner in the mistaken belief that these things are unbreakable. They are, in fact, breakable. And expensive to replace.

Do not nibble on your ingredients or stuff your face in the kitchen while preparing your meal and before sitting down at the dinner table. For example, do not eat all the Parmesan cheese you just shredded, or else you will get full and there will be no more shredded Parmesan to cook with.

Do not despair of your failures in the beginning. Do not underestimate that cooking needs a lot of practice. It might take years—but it is worth it.

According to experts, making toast does not count as cooking. The same is true for ordering take-away and using a can opener.

Avoid squeezing a lemon if you have a paper cut on your finger.

Cooking is about passion. If you do not enjoy it or are not having fun, do not do it!

Do not believe the use-by dates on all your food. They are put there by lawyers. Ordinary humans are much more resilient than the law would have you believe. Test results on self first, twenty-four hours before fobbing off on family and friends.

Do not cook when you are angry—your dishes will be furious too!

Do not cook when you are hungry.

Do not put hot beverages near your hard drive or you might have to replace your hard drive.

Do not smoke when cooking!

Do not sneeze or cough in front of your dish or ingredients.

Do not start cooking when you are already too hungry.

Do not store cookbooks in the oven.

Do not stress! It is all about putting love in your food.

Do not surrender to any dish you are cooking. If something fails, do your best to rescue it.

Do not fall into the trap of refining canned or frozen dinners and believe you can sell this for cooking.

Do not taste your food with the same utensil that you are using to cook with.

Do not try to make Beef Stroganoff if you are feeling even slightly emotional—it is a trigger food. There are certain tricky parts to the recipe that will set you off if you get them wrong, and if you screw up the whole thing the ingredients are mighty expensive. It will make you cry, and cry, and cry.

Do not wear your hair loose.

Do not leave home very young or you will be hungry. Do not wish to make bread and forget to add yeast. Do not attempt to copy illustrations of kneading techniques and wonder if this is how it should be. Bake until done. Enjoy breadlike aroma. Do not attempt to consume bricklike product by moistening with last remaining reconstituted tin of Campbell's concentrated mushroom soup. Consume soup, scraping last drops off concrete croutons. Be hungry.

Even when cooking simple things like ground beef, stews, scones, and shortbread, take your time, and do not forget when you have put something on the burner.

If a dish has turned out to be no success, do not throw it out the window. Your neighbors will not appreciate this.

If you are lucky enough to remember all of the ingredients, but then forget the cooking time, you were probably born to eat out.

If you do not like to cook, it will be tasted in the food.

Do not not cook! It has a lot of advantages and time is always well invested: It is a form of meditation and thus will increase happiness. It contributes to your state of health. You can give a lot of love to your friends and family by cooking. You are more attractive to potential sexual partners. You are a better parent. And you're more likely to survive a war, based on my grandmother, who is a skilled cook.

If you ever get to whip mayonnaise yourself, offer it your most beautiful thoughts. Give it compliments and let it know it is the best mayonnaise ever to be beaten! Never do it in a bad or sad mood—it will not rise!

Never be barefoot when you are chopping, cooking, or doing anything in the kitchen, or you might get a knife stuck in your foot.

Never cook with too much enthusiasm!

Never eat something that just came out of the oven, a casserole, or a pan. It is probably going to be too hot to taste and you will burn your hands, lips, tongue, or palate, thus ruining every actual chance of enjoying anything you cooked.

Ordering take-out for dinner is not a sin. Ordering take-out for breakfast is.

Show no fear when cooking. Do not worry too much; if you do, you will skimp on putting enough ingredients in and experimenting. Who cares if the carrots are a bit crunchy? You can taste when a meal has been cooked with passion and confidence, and it is more nourishing.

When cooking for people who live in a residential home, do not forget how much they will enjoy a choice of three meals for lunch.

When learning to cook you are told—with love and hope—that you are sure to make wonderful dishes as long as you taste your creations as you go. What they do not tell you is that you are also sure to end up with a waistline that fills your kitchen from counter to sink!

When preparing a meal, do not think about someone you dislike. Also be aware of all the effort and human toil that have made the ingredients available to you.

You can talk while you are cooking but never have a conversation. A conversation is communication among two, three, or more people, but talking only uses the mouth. Although a conversation, like cooking, must have a specific balance to be successful, a successful conversation will represent a failure in cooking. Either you burn something, administer too much of something, or you forget to add a necessary ingredient. This is not the time to practice your social skills. So whether you like it or not, whether you enjoy more than anything sharing the process with others, do share drinks, snacks, a helping hand—but never establish a conversation.

Marinades

Apparently putting things in water does not count as marinating.

Do not marinate chicken pieces in a mayonnaise-based marinade and then assume that putting them under the broiler with vast quantities of excess marinade will increase the tastiness. The chicken will be no tastier, and the marinade will catch on fire.

Oh, my God! Do not take fine, pure ingredients such as leg of lamb, garlic, and honey and imagine that they go together! You will make an expensive mistake combining the latter two into a glaze—it will taste like vomit. If meat is murder (but tasty murder), then this is genocide. Do not!

When grilling meat, do not use a sweet marinade such as Indonesian soy or Japanese mirin. The sugars will carbonize like a meteor well before your meat is sufficiently cooked. If you want a sweet glaze, baste over low heat in the last few minutes of cooking.

When grilling, do not use barbeque sauce until the meat is almost done, as the sugars in it will burn.

When roasting a pork or lamb leg, do not season at the time of cooking; let it rest overnight with a flavorful marinade.

Meat 'n Potatoes

If you hit yourself and it hurts, put some raw meat on the bruise. It will ease the pain. Do not cover it with a Ziploc bag; what you need is the raw, bloody meat.

Never put potatoes in boiling water. Put them in cold water and then start boiling.

Do not take meat out of the trash can and use it in a meal you are serving up to friends, especially if your friends are watching you.

If your piece of meat falls on the ground, do not forget to also put the other side on the floor before cooking it. This way it will have the same taste on both sides!

Try to avoid serving mashed potato with custard. It is not a good combination.

When grilling meat Argentinean style, add some kosher salt to your fire. If you do not add salt, the carbon monoxide that comes out of your charcoal will go into your meat.

When grilling meats that have bone, like ribs, put the bone side on the grill. Do not place the meat side on the grill. This way you will cook the meat from the bone up and it will not get burnt.

Do not salt your meat before frying, or it will turn chewy. Always do it afterward.

Do not microwave a baking potato for more than fifteen minutes unless you are trying to make charcoal. It stinks.

Do not add salt to the meat before cooking; this will make your meat get a shoe sole texture.

When cooking meatloaf, avoid leaving it for more than thirty-five minutes in the oven—unless you like dry meat.

Do not attempt to microwave a Pork Escalope coated in egg and breadcrumbs instead of pan-frying it. Thinking that this will make it a healthier option is no consolation for the fact that the egg and breadcrumbs just slide off and the escalope goes all chewy.

Do not check the steak every fifteen seconds. Do not perpetually flip it from side to side.

Do not cook bacon in the microwave or it will be chewy.

Do not cook hamburgers in muffin pans.

Do not cook your potatoes without letting them sit in cold water beforehand.

Do not, under any circumstances, ever cook sausages in a microwave. If you do, you deserve to eat rock-hard, sadly anemic-looking sausages, which is exactly the way they will turn out.

Do not forget to use eggs in the bread mixture for Vitello Milanese.

Do not fry your potatoes with fatty ingredients. You want your potatoes to be crusty, not fatty.

Do not grate raw potatoes directly into the pan with a fine rasp thinking that it is going to be faster. What you get is a chewing gum–like mass.

Do not leave meat in the oven. Even if you turn the oven off, the meat will continue to cook.

Do not make Shish Kabobs for a large number of people; it takes too long to cut and assemble the sticks.

Do not microwave hamburgers.

Do not put potatoes in the oven without salt.

Do not salt your meat right before cooking it or it will dry up. It will also take all the taste away.

Do not serve steak right after you are done cooking it.

Do not tell your guests where you have bought the meat. So what if the lamb is from the supermarket?

Do not try to make mashed potatoes with an electric hand blender or you will end up with wallpaper paste.

Do not try to shorten cooking time of a roast by increasing the temperature. The outcome is almost necessarily a burned rather than roasted piece of meat, not to speak of its chewy consistency.

Do not use colored string to tie up your meat when roasting. The dye will most likely run into the meat and turn it a funny color.

If you are cooking Gratin Potatoes and you want to prep ahead, slice the potatoes but never put them in the fridge! Leave them in cold water to prevent them from going black.

If you are making Potato Gnocchi, use what are known as black potatoes or baking potatoes, never boiling potatoes. Boiling potatoes, when mashed, tend to be thick and very lumpy, and for gnocchi you need the mash light and creamy.

If your Spinach Gnocchi does not solidify, you are often left with a basin of green slop.

If you are using vegetables and meats in your dish, do not cut them on the same boards and do not use the same knives. Raw meat, if handled by amateurs, can become a health hazard—so keep your raw vegetables away from your raw meat.

If you have bought a nice T-bone, try using a good knife to cut it. Do not use a serrated knife, since this will break its fibers and make it lose its juiciness.

If you prepare Stoofvlees or Carbonade Flamande, which is a Flemish beef stew cooked in beer, do not forget to chose the right type of dark brown Belgian beer. With a blond beer, the whole plate turns acidic and you will have to throw it all away.

If your stew is salty, do not give up, just add a potato. It will suck all the salt out.

If your stew is too salty, add more water. Do not add a potato. The potato will draw the liquid, not the salt.

Just like when you use a pan, calculate the amount of food you will place over the barbeque. Do not try to fit a lot of food on it or some of it will burn and some will be raw.

Do not just compress ground meat in making your own hamburger! Make sure to mix the meat with egg yolk, because it will act as a binder.

We all love hamburgers and everything that goes with them, but remember that lettuce is the fresh and cold part of your burger, so do not grill the lettuce.

When asked to prepare potato salad for a large family picnic, do not forget to bear in mind that the potatoes must first be cooked—boiled, baked, or roasted.

When cooking a pot roast, do not wait until the last forty-five minutes to throw the vegetables and potatoes in around the roast; they will not be done in time.

When cooking a sauerkraut stew, do not boil the potatoes together with the sauerkraut. They will not get done.

When cooking meat, do not cut into it to have a sneak preview to see how it is cooked. Instead, lightly press your right index finger against your right thumb, and then with your left index finger prod the fleshy part of your hand beneath your thumb. This signifies the rare consistency of the steak you are cooking. Now prod the meat to compare with your own flesh and you will notice the visceral similarity. Middle finger denotes medium-rare, ring finger medium, and little finger well-done.

When cooking meat, do not add salt, because it draws out the meat's juices.

When making French Fries, leave them soaking for ten minutes in water. But do not fry them while wet. Instead, make sure they are dry when you fry them or your fryer will cause an oil eruption.

When frying a steak, do not turn it with a fork; always use a gripper or spatula. Otherwise the juice will leak out of the holes made by the fork, and the meat will dry up.

When frying meat, never cook it in a cold pan. Always cook it in warm fat.

When making French Fries, do not cook on super-high heat—the potatoes will turn brown and will be soggy.

When making French Fries, if you throw the cut potatoes into the oil before it heats up high enough, your fries will be soggy and soft.

When making Stovies, do not use instant mashed potatoes; it does not taste very nice—best to go with the real thing.

When preparing potatoes for a special heart-shaped Valentine's Day Rösti, do not, in your enthusiasm, grate them in the morning and then put them in the fridge without covering them in salted water. Otherwise they will turn black, and your dinner may be ruined. Fortunately couscous is a quick, easy alternative. You still may get brownie points for trying so hard.

When trying to fix a stew or something that is oversalted, do not just add water, because it will lose its flavor. Add a raw potato, which will absorb some of the saltiness, and add a raw onion, which will add some sweetness.

When you are making meatballs, do not just use breadcrumbs. You should also add some bread soaked with milk so that the meatballs will not be dry.

When you are preparing liver dishes, never salt the liver beforehand or it will get hard.

When you refrigerate fried potatoes, do not cover the pan or they will become soggy.

Melanzane
(Eggplant)

If you want to fry eggplant successfully, do not cook it without preparing the eggplant first. You must drain the black acid water out of it and salt it; otherwise it will be utterly unflavorful.

Do not forget to salt the eggplant before cooking. This will take out some of the water. If you forget, the eggplant will become very little and dry when you fry them.

If you do not want super-oily eggplant, do not put the eggplant slices facedown after frying. Put a small bowl upside down in a larger bowl and then line up the eggplant in vertical strips with the sides of the eggplant resting on the large bowl and the tip of the eggplant resting on the small bowl. This way the oil will drain out of the eggplant.

Never fry eggplant without soaking them first in water with salt.

When making Melanzane Ammuttunate, never use basil.

When working as an assistant cook at a school, you might forget to cut the eggplants thinly and then cook them slowly in hot oil. They will come out like black rubber.

Do not use Sicilian eggplants for Caponata. Always use Tunisian eggplants, because they are milder and sweeter.

Menstruation

Do not make mayonnaise when you have your period. It will go bad.

Do not cook pulses when you are premenstrual. Many women have a tendency to burn pulses when they are premenstrual.

My mother used to say that if you have your period, do not try to pickle green beans. When you are cooking them they turn muddy and the pickle jars do not close. I do not know if this is true, as nobody pickles beans these days.

Do not try to make mayonnaise when you have your period—it will not set. If you really want to have a go, though, make sure that all the ingredients are at the same temperature. That way you will have more chance of succeeding.

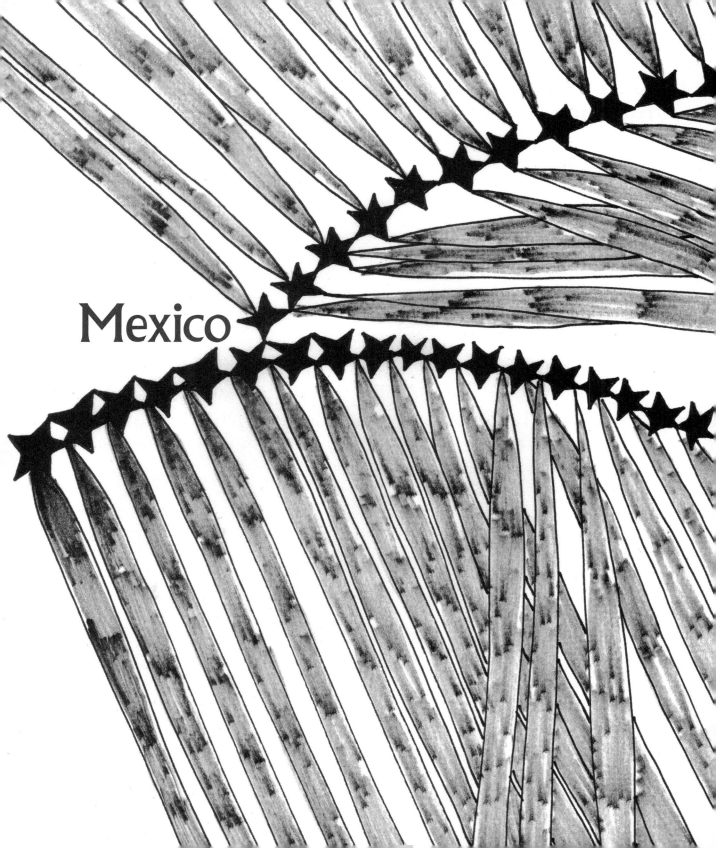

Mexico

If you are frying pumpkin, yucca, or yautía, make sure to do it in a pan with very hot oil. Do not use warm oil or you will have soggy fritters.

Do not complicate your Guacamole. The simpler, the better. Use mashed Hass avocados, a bit of chopped onion, some cilantro, one to three chiles, salt, a squeezed lemon to prevent it from going black, and the bone of the avocado will do. Different cultures make their own variations. In Guadalajara, some people add pomegranate; in some regions of Mexico, nopalitos (cactus); in Japan, wasabi, seaweed, soy sauce, and sesame seeds; in Costa Rica, coconut; in Italy, pine nuts, basil, and olive oil; in England, mint. The great lesson of Guacamole is that almost everything can be mixed together but if you want to make politically correct Guacamole, do not try doing it with avocados coming from Israel mixed with cilantro from Palestine, or Mexican avocados with tomatoes grown in the USA by migrant workers. The best way to eat Guacamole is rolled in a taco made of soft, just-made corn tortilla, which might be difficult to find. Doritos or flour tortillas are acceptable substitutes. Blue corn tortillas are a sophisticated eccentricity. But do not ever prepare it the USA way, where they add sour cream or Philadelphia Cream Cheese and let it cool down in the refrigerator. Do not add tomatoes; it makes the Guacamole soggy.

Do not add lemon to raw fish if you intend to cook it afterward. This will cook the fish and if you recook it later it will be rubbery. If you add lemon you will have Ceviche. Better to save the lemon for later and put it on the plate—do not assume everyone loves lemon with their fish.

Do not fry homemade Taquitos in extra-virgin olive oil—use canola oil. The olive oil will make them more oily and overpower the taste.

Do not make your burrito too thick.

If you are doing Brochetas, do not fry everything at the same time, and remember that pepper is good for the memory—you will remember you ate it every time you repeat it.

When cooking Mexican tortillas, remember to buy the appropriate flour rather than substitute with fine white cornstarch, which is all the convenience stores have in stock. It will take considerable time to clean up the gluey mess if you do end up using this flour!

If you drink Maté, never prepare it with boiling water because it burns the leaves and it becomes really bitter. Make it with very hot water and remember that unlike most teas, Maté can be steeped many, many times—it is part of the tradition. Oh, and please, do not add milk—it is not English Breakfast Tea. Do not get creative with tradition.

If you make Guacamole, do not throw out the avocado pit. Instead put it in the mix to prevent the Guacamole from going black.

If you use Mexican tortillas or the American imitation, preheat them. If you do not preheat them, your tortilla will not be warm and easy to handle, and it will burn while the cheese in your Quesadilla is melting.

When making Mexican Red Rice, after frying it and letting it brown, add the tomato puree and cook until it dries. Do not pour in the water until the tomato is completely absorbed by the rice—this way you will enjoy a bright red and flavorful rice.

When doing Paella Valenciana, do not forget to cover it with a wet cloth and change it from time to time if you want it to be well cooked.

When making caramel for your flan, make sure to melt your sugar until it is golden brown, not black—never black. If it goes black it means the sugar is burned and the caramel will be bitter instead of sweet.

There are some meals that are better from a can, rather than cooked at home—for example, abalone. Unless you like exercising your jaws.

POEM:

Hello Beautiful —
it's alright to cry.

Milk

Do not heat chocolate milk in an electric kettle, because the milk bakes onto the element and flakes into your tea forevermore.

Do not add too much milk and cream cheese to your Mashed Potatoes or they will be completely pasty. Yuck.

Do not leave the kitchen when you are heating milk. Milk burns very quickly.

Do not put a tea bag in boiling water or anything in boiling milk. It will burble over and burn you and you will not have much liquid left in your cup.

Do not warm up milk and have a shower while it is heating. You will ruin your breakfast by doing this.

Do not tell your guests how you make Kefir before offering it to them.

Do not use the toaster to heat up milk.

If you are a super-hungry fitness freak who wakes up when your stomach tells you to and are about to prepare breakfast in your favorite big glass salad mixing bowl, adding ingredients for your super-satisfying, totally organic breakfast Müesli mix of traditional oats, a handful of hand-crushed walnuts, some crushed almonds, Brazil nuts, hazelnuts, cashews, shelled hemp seeds, raisins, sunflower seeds, pumpkin seeds, a sliced banana, an expertly cut-up apple, a handful of green grapes, another of black grapes, and finally a generous handful of delicious sliced strawberries—be careful when you add the milk. You will be extremely hungry, almost dribbling when you take out the carton from the fridge, shake it up, and pour it all into the bowl, gazing lovingly at the kaleidoscope of colors and textures before your eyes. The bowl will be full. It will be a feast in a bowl. You will give it a stir with your favorite big-mouthful spoon and take the pot containing the rainbow to the breakfast bar and sit down. The first mouthful of lovingly prepared breakfast will reveal the criminally foul taste of milk that has gone off. Badly. In disbelief you will tentatively try another. Yes, the milk is badly off. You will be very unhappy. And yet even when you put the whole mixture into a sieve, drain off the milk and wash all of the ingredients in fresh water and add new fresh milk you will know that the taste of rancid milk has already got into everything. Your desperate cries of injustice will never be answered. Why did you not sniff the milk first? You will want to break something, but instead, disgusted with the world, you will then make some toast.

If you want to heat up milk for your breakfast, remember to turn the gas on.

The ability to create coffee with soy milk is not increased by reading online forum discussions providing top tips on how to make the two blend together. It is simply easier to buy a soy milk coffee in a hip vegan café for an astoundingly expensive fee than experiment with stirring techniques and various milk temperatures at home.

When cooking rice pudding, do not turn your back to the stove, not even for an instant. The milk will feel neglected and do what it can to get your attention, and you will have a lot of hot milk to wash off your hotplates.

When scrambling an egg, it is an undeniably common misconception that it is necessary to add milk. The recipe requires an egg or two depending on hunger, a small amount of butter or cream (never both), and salt and pepper added at the end. Bring a skillet to medium temperature and add in ingredients and continuously stir with a wooden spoon until preferred consistency is achieved. Do not add milk, as the method and taste will be inextricably altered for the worse.

When heating milk, be careful that it does not spill when it boils, but also do not take too much care of it while heating. It will never boil until you turn somewhere else.

Navigation

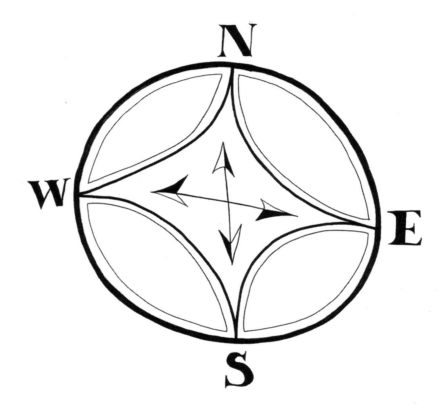

Remember that the longer the cook keeps the crew waiting, the hungrier they are. Therefore, the faster they eat, the less bad cooking they taste.

When cooking on a boat, ensure that you use the fresh water supply and not the bilge pump to fill your pans.

When on a boat away from land for many months, you will discover that powdered eggs are useful for all kinds of dishes and desserts. But do not attempt to make a chocolate mousse with powdered eggs.

While sailing, do not try to prepare or cook quiche, flan, or anything liquid based, because the motion of the boat (especially if the helmsman tacks without letting the cook know) will slosh your egg and liquid ingredients all over the galley floor or interior of the oven—if you even make it that far.

Nuts

If you are making nut butter in a blender or food processor and your nuts are resisting the step from flour to butter consistency, do not try to help them along by adding water. Your nut butter will be tasteless and will likely grow mold within a couple weeks.

Do not put walnuts into chutney if you are canning it. They will turn soft and purple, like creatures in formaldehyde jars.

Do not combine protein and nuts.

Do not eat raw almonds, unless you take the skin off.

Do not try to peel almonds with a knife. It takes about thirty minutes and two bleeding fingertips to peel about four almonds. Rather, scald with boiling water and peel off the skin easily. This is also advisable for peeling tomatoes as well as other fruits and vegetables.

Orientalism

Never cook Chinese food with full-sized ingredients. Make sure they are cut to bite-sized pieces. Since only chopsticks are to be used for eating, you would not want to have to use your teeth to tear big pieces apart. It is also practical to cut the food smaller, as it is then also faster to cook.

Do not forget to closely read the label when purchasing the sweet cooking wine called mirin. It is traditionally made from fermented mochigome rice and shochu liquor, but is often sold with corn syrup as the main ingredient.

Do not just crack a raw egg into a bowl of semi-hot vegetables and rice and hope that it will cook up and taste like Bibimbap in a hot stone bowl. It is simply not possible.

Do not let homemade Kombucha ferment for more than ten days with the mother, or it will taste like pure vinegar.

If making korean curry, do not cut the meat and vegetables into pieces that are too small—with small pieces it will not have the same taste.

If you prepare Shrimp Pad Thai only from time to time and the peanut oil has been sitting in your pantry for a couple of months already, do not add it before trying it first in order to avoid the whole dish tasting like rancid peanuts.

If you want to prepare a real Asian meal, do not mix dishes from different regions such as Fried Rice and Sushi and Spring Rolls. It is a culinary and cultural sacrilege!

Never cook Chinese with electric cooking plates. In order to achieve wok hei—the flavor, tastes, and essence in Chinese cuisine—cook only with gas. Only with gas can the food be cooked with high heat and speed, resulting in caramelization and the texture and smells described as the wok hei.

To create wasabi paste, never start by adding your wasabi powder to water. Always put a small amount of the powder first on the plate, then use slow dripping water to mix the powder to the right amount. If you start with water first, you have to pour enough powder to absorb the water and may end up with more wasabi than you need.

When making Tibetan Momo, close the dough completely and do not leave any holes.

When preparing Sushi, do not put water on the nori sheet at the beginning of the process, as this will cause the nori to disintegrate. After the filling process, only enough water should be brushed along the inside edge to seal the roll.

When using Japanese ingredients such as miso and soy sauce, make sure they are made in a traditional way, preferably organic and without preservatives and colorings. These products are extremely healthy and taste much better than their industrially produced equivalents. Do not miss the chance of getting good health from your food!

Pasta

Avoid mixing butter and oil when preparing a pasta dish—it makes the pasta inedible!

Do not add oil or butter to the pasta water, because the grease will seal the surface of the pasta, which makes it impossible for the sauce to stick to it.

Do not add oil or butter to your pasta if you are already making a sauce. It will just make your dish too heavy.

Do not add oil to the water for cooking pasta. Sauce will not cling to oil-coated pasta.

Do not forget to add salt to the pasta water.

Do not forget to put salt and a bit of oil in the pasta water you are boiling.

Do not put salt in pasta water if it is boiling fast. It could boil even faster, come out of the pot, and burn you.

Do not add salt to the pasta water before it boils. Some people think that when you add salt after the water is boiling, it will lower the temperature of the boiling water so they add salt to the cold water and then boil it. This is a common misconception. Adding salt to water that is already boiling does no harm.

When cooking pasta, it is very common to add some oil to the pot with the boiling water. For some purposes this is okay, but never do this if you are going to serve pasta with a sauce. The reason is that after you strain it, the pasta absorbs all the oil from the top of the pot and the sauce will not blend very well but will slip away from the spaghetti.

Do not attempt to test the readiness of your spaghetti by throwing it at a ceiling that is significantly higher than your height or the height of you + your tallest chair. If your spaghetti is in fact cooked, it may not come down until the ceiling does.

Do not leave pasta in a pan or a pot, because it will keep cooking. Always transfer it to a platter for serving.

Do not make Pasta Salmone with three people. There will be three times too much onion.

Do not forget that your pasta is cooking.

Do not overcook pasta or all the fatty elements will be released, and hence eating pasta will be unhealthy. If you cook it just right—that, is al dente—it will be fine and healthy. Well, only if you eat it in moderation, of course!

Do not overcook the pasta in unsalted water.

Do not put pasta in cold water in a small pot. Always wait for the pasta water to boil and use a big pot so that the pasta has space.

Do not run your noodles under cold water and then heat them up again.

Do not rinse the pasta under cold water when it is done.

Do not serve bread with pasta.

Do not serve mushy pasta. If you ruined your pasta and it is not al dente, just sauté it in olive oil or butter for a few minutes.

Do not serve pasta in flat plates.

Do not start making a pasta sauce once you have already started cooking the pasta—it will never be ready on time.

Do not throw cooked pasta against the kitchen wall to test if it is al dente. It is a myth that it will stick against the wall. Most likely it will only make your kitchen look more dirty, and it will make you look like a lunatic throwing pasta around.

Do not throw your spaghetti on the ceiling to test whether it is cooked. Taste it or look at the instructions on the packet.

Do not try the "spaghetti on the ceiling" trick more than once. Or, if you have to do it, at least use a new strand of the spaghetti if the first has already fallen to the floor.

When making Tagliatelle al Limon, do not boil the cream together with the acidic lemon juice. They will separate, and this cannot be undone.

If you have made or bought fresh pasta for dinner and the dampness of the day has made all the ravioli stick together in one block, do not try to pry the shapes apart; you will just break the pasta. If you put the block into the boiling water as is, the ravioli will probably separate.

Never boil fresh pasta like ravioli or tortellini without rolling them in flour first. If you forget they will split open in the water.

If you rarely see your family and you lie to them about your cooking experience, inviting them to an Easter Sunday Spaghetti and Clam dinner that you say you have prepared a million times before, you might end up keeping them waiting for hours because you simply forgot to wash the soft Mediterranean sand off of the clams. It will be pointless to try to cover up this mistake. When your brother finally tastes the spaghetti he will spit the food out. Everyone will complain, while your mother will have no choice but to make pasta with nothing but butter for everyone that night.

Never boil water for pasta in a pan. It needs a lot of space.

Never cook pasta at a simmer, and never in too little water. The pasta will not cook properly, because it will not get to free its starch and it will turn soft very quickly without you noticing. In Italian the word is *scuocere*—literally "uncook"!

Never cook spaghetti in its entire length, because you will need a fork and spoon to eat it.

Never heat Pesto Sauce. Basil will turn black and the sauce will taste bitter. What should be hot is the pasta, not the Pesto.

Never use packaged ravioli. Ravioli has to be handmade and fresh.

Pasta gains neither in taste nor in style when cooked for too long. If you try cooking it for about an hour you will end up with properly mashed pasta.

When cooked, pasta will stick to walls and ceilings. Do not be tempted, like many students are, to throw pasta at high walls and ceilings to test its readiness. It will accumulate rapidly as if by magic and will require high stepladders and a scraper to remove it. Redecoration will be necessary unless you want to retain the effect and paint over it.

When cooking pasta, do not go and sit in front of the TV or play video games while waiting for it to cook. Most likely you will forget about it and you will be eating overboiled Chinese noodles for dinner.

When cooking pasta, do not let it sit and warm in the pot or it will get soggy. Do not rinse pasta in cold water—this removes the whole point of pasta, which is to bind itself to a sauce. An overcooked rinsed pasta cannot support anything.

When cooking pasta with a wooden spoon, do not leave it inside the pot. If you like eating pasta often, you will run out of spoons very soon.

When cooking pasta, use salt and not oil to stop it from sticking. Oil will stop the pasta from sticking to itself, but it will also stop any sauce from sticking to the pasta. Salt does only the former.

When making Carbonara from scratch, do not leave the pan on the heat when adding the egg mixture—or you will end up with a lovely plate of something which resembles spaghetti and scrambled eggs!

When making Macaroni and Cheese, do not forget to add the flour to the mixture so it becomes a cheese and milk sauce.

When making Macaroni and Cheese, do not forget to drain the pasta before adding the sauce or it will create a congealed watery cheese sauce and the pan will need soaking for two days.

When making Spaghetti Bolognese while at the same time entertaining friends, do not absentmindedly substitute lemon dishwashing liquid for olive oil. This will produce a strange bubbling effect and a citrus aroma, the reason for which you will have trouble determining, until noticing the proximity of the squeeze bottle to the stove. Naturally the Bolognese will have to be consigned to that great macerator in the sky.

When making Tuna Pasta, do not fry an onion and a clove of garlic in some oil until it is slightly bitter and black around the edges, as it will impart a nasty edge to this budget meal. Adding a can of drained tuna in brine, a can of chopped tomatoes, and a tablespoon of tomato puree, do not simmer for fifteen minutes until it is slightly solid, to then blend through some pasta.

When preparing a pasta dish, be sure to check that the pasta is not infested with weevils before cooking. Also remember to keep the packaging, as to be able to note the brand and inform someone of a serious quarantine issue.

When preparing Spaghetti Aglio e Olio, the garlic should be cut in slices and cooked to a very golden stage—almost crunchy. When the pasta is very al dente, turn off the sauce and throw in a handful of chopped parsley. The spaghetti should not be drained but lifted out of the pot straight into the pan with the sauce. The excess water will create a great balance.

When rolling out dough for fresh pasta, do not forget to put flour on the rolling pin and a little oil on your fingers to help flatten out the pasta.

When your pasta water is boiling, do not forget to add some kosher salt and a pinch of olive oil. This will prevent your pasta from sticking.

You cannot always have a clear sink all the time, but always make sure you have enough space to drain your pasta; otherwise you might well overcook it or burn yourself.

You do not have to stir pasta constantly. Always stir it at the beginning, when you first add the pasta.

Fresh pasta should be stirred more often than dry pasta.

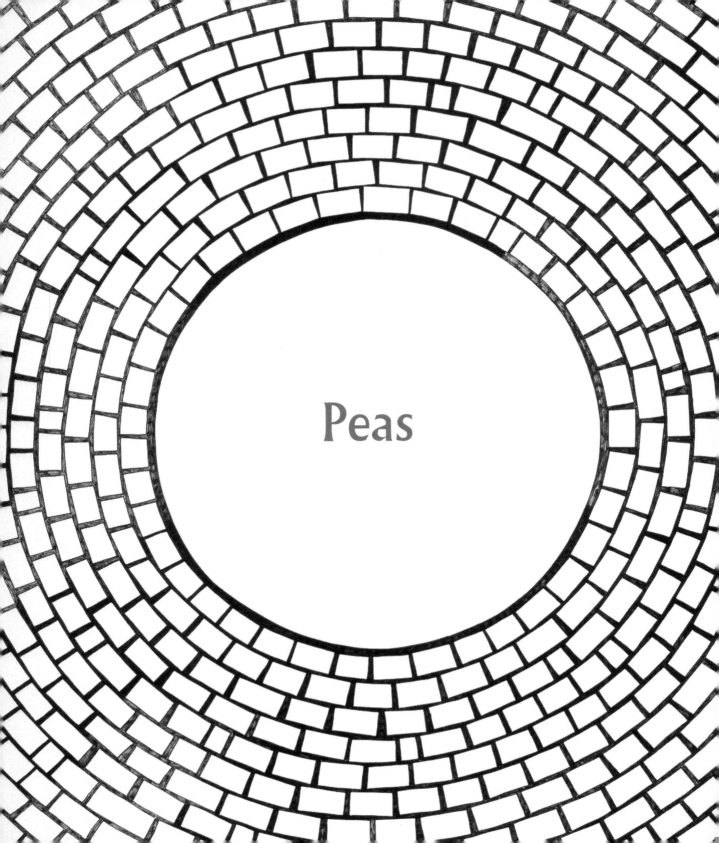

Peas

Do not cook chickpeas without soaking them. If you forget they will come out like mothballs.

Do not add bicarbonate of soda and salt to beans when you soak them.

Do not drain garden peas with the saucepan lid on; it is always safer to use a colander.

Do not put beans on to boil while doing other things like checking if the laundry is ready. You might leave your keys inside the apartment and not only will your beans burn, but you may also find your apartment in flames.

Do not forget to add bicarbonate to beans if you want a rich texture.

Do not forget to rinse canned beans especially well. Removing the preservatives will help lessen the flatulence factor.

Do not stop eating beans due to flatulence or other discomfort—they are very good for you. The best way is to allow the beans to sprout for two or three days and then cook them as usual. They will be much easier to digest and their enzymes will also be increased.

Do not think that Boston Baked Beans are a good addition to a curry.

Good intentions aside, do not make veggie patties two days before you plan to fry them. Lentils + rice = complex carbohydrates and proteins which break down in your kitchen, not your stomach. This dilemma no amount of oil or spices can resolve.

What not to do with soy or any other dried beans—cover them in water until they become foamy and smelly and then throw them away.

When cooking beans, soften them in water for three days, changing the water from time to time.

When cooking fresh fava beans, do not use a metal spoon to stir the beans, because the beans will turn dark brown. You have to use a wooden spoon.

When you are newlywed and you and your spouse experiment with a range of recipes from many different cultures, do not just follow the instructions for Chili con Carne and soak dried red kidney beans to make the dish, or you might become violently sick. Do not forget to use only canned red kidney beans to make chili!

Pets

If you have a cat, close your kitchen door while you cook. If not, you could end up cat-less or dinner-less.

Do not bake with your cat in the kitchen. When baking a sponge cake for your son's primary-school fair, you may put both halves out to cool. When you come back the cake will be gone. Part of one of the halves will be on the floor and the other half will have disappeared, while your Burmese cat is having a wash innocently not far away. You will then have to bake another cake and it will now be very late at night. You might get as far as icing and putting the new cake in a tin with the lid off. Then you will go away to answer the phone and you will hear a crash—your cat has knocked the tin on the floor and is pawing at the new cake.

Do not play or pet your animals in the kitchen. Hair, dirt—and in the worst case ticks and fleas—can end up in your ingredients, cooking utensils, and food.

Do not underestimate the gustatory appreciation of other mammals than yourself—rodents are fine eaters too! Do not leave a mess in your kitchen, especially on the floor.

Do not waste food. All food can be put to some use, even leftovers. Food scraps make great treats for the cats and dogs.

When cooking sausages, remember to contain the cat!

When making Banoffee Pie from a recipe which calls for two cans of condensed milk to be boiled in a pan, do not think there is enough water in the pan to stop it from boiling dry, and then go out for a while. When you come back you will realize that the water has boiled away, the gas is still on, and the cans have exploded. The explosion of hot caramel will cover the kitchen walls, window, ceiling, and your poor cat.

When making risotto, do not decide to follow a recipe that was created for the chef's dog in need of a balanced diet of carbohydrates and protein. Adding barley to a ground turkey risotto will result in a meal that is startlingly reminiscent of eating warm sleeping bag padding or soggy cat litter.

Poultry

When popcorn stuffing a turkey, do not assume unpopped popcorn kernels will just pop inside the turkey. They will not, and your Thanksgiving guests will break their teeth.

Do not cook a chicken without first removing the rubber band from around its legs and the plastic bag of the giblets from inside.

Do not cook the gizzards inside the chicken.

Do not forget to check the cavity of your chicken or turkey. The small plastic bag containing liver and heart is not a lucky dip for your dinner guests. It is intended to be used to make a gravy and should be removed before putting the bird in the oven to roast.

Do not serve rabbit to guests without telling them what it is—if you forget, they will only think that it is chicken.

Do not cook a turkey without aluminum foil on the breast or it will dry out and most likely burn.

Do not deep-fry a frozen turkey.

If making a turkey for Christmas that is far too big for the refrigerator, do not leave it out in the garage until Christmas morning. If you do, after hours of cooking it will turn out looking like one of the lions in Trafalgar Square.

If you cook a Christmas turkey with the plastic still on, and the giblets inside, do not tell your guests. Pop some tinfoil on top and serve it regardless.

Make sure you separate your food into portions before you freeze it. That bumper pack of ten chicken breasts may have been a bargain, but you will not be as happy when you try to separate off a single portion with a hammer and a chisel. In the end you may have to defrost the whole lot and eat nothing but chicken for the following week.

Never boil a pigeon before roasting it.

Never use high heat for chicken and peppers. They need to be cooked very slowly. If you use high heat they will be burnt on the outside and uncooked on the inside.

Preparing the Christmas goose should include a meticulous search for any overlooked feathers at the very start. If left on the bird, they will react with the heat of the stove. If you then try to burn them off with a candle while the guests are already lining up in the corridor, you will leave lumps of lilac wax all over the crisp skin of the bird.

When baking a turkey, do not forget to take out the bag of innards. It is not an appetizing treasure to find on Thanksgiving.

When cooking a turkey, do not forget to check the inside of the bird; sometimes there is a bag with viscera inside, and you do not want melted plastic on your bird.

When cooking poultry, do it exactly like steak. Make a small incision on the thicker part of your meat so it can bleed while cooking. Sear it on high and then cook it on low for about fifteen to twenty minutes, depending on how juicy you want it. Otherwise you will end up eating bloody, health-threatening, raw chicken.

Do not forget to flay the hare before roasting it. In contrast to freshly butchered poultry, the skin is not singed off.

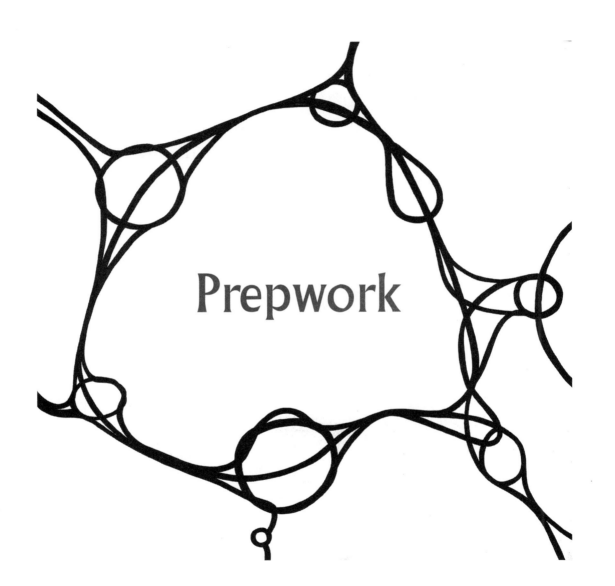

Prepwork

Do not chop onions and garlic on the same cutting board that you use to chop up fruit! If you do, your strawberries will end up tasting like armpits!

Always check that all recipe ingredients have made it into the mix before putting anything in the oven. If not, you might realize too late that an essential ingredient has been left out, or is still sitting on the scale pan.

Do not cook without washing your hands beforehand.

Do not cut artichokes unless you already have boiling water ready to cook them in; otherwise they will go black while you wait for the water to boil.

Do not cut your vegetables at the same time as cooking.

Do not forget that if you are touching poultry or fish, wash your hands before touching anything else.

Do not forget to chop ingredients according to their role in a given dish. For example, if onions are meant to add flavor and serve as a subtle ingredient, they should be chopped finely, while mushrooms—if the centerpiece of a dish—should be left in bigger pieces. Either way, the ingredients should all be different sizes; it keeps the dish from being one-dimensional and aesthetically boring.

Do not forget to wash your hands!

Do not prepare your ingredients as you are already cooking.

Do not put the whole contents of your refrigerator in your recipe. Think before cooking.

Do not sharpen other people's knives for them when cooking in their kitchen, especially without telling them you have done so.

Do not test how sharp your knife is by using the tip of your finger.

Do not use a dull knife. Never. Ever.

Do not use blunt knives—they are more dangerous than sharp ones.

It is always better to oil or butter your food than your pan or grill. When using a barbeque, do not oil or butter just the pan—do both to prevent food from sticking.

NEVER ever use a knife with wet hands.

Tidy up your kitchen, line up your ingredients, get your tools ready, study and follow your recipe—but do not let organization kill your passion.

When cleaning strong meats like goat and lamb, do not use water. Instead use white vinegar, an orange, or a lemon instead. Tap water in most countries contains chlorine and it will actually accentuate that strong flavor.

When cutting onions, breathe through your mouth and not your nose. Your eyes will not tear as much.

When making a variety of dishes for dinner, figure out how long each dish will take to make, so you can time them. You do not want one food to get cold while waiting for the other. Reheated food is not as good. Do not forget to take into account preparation time, not just cooking time.

When preparing an avocado to use in cooking do not imitate chefs on TV and stab at the pit with a knife to remove it. The knife may slip off the pit and needless to say you will be in the emergency room right after!

When you are chopping loads of ingredients for a stir-fry, soup, or stew, start with the ingredient that takes the least time to cook. Put it at the bottom of a big bowl, then chop the other ingredients in reverse order of cooking time. When you are done, the ingredients will be ready to put into the pan as you need them. For example, cut mushrooms, then zucchini, then red pepper, then carrot, then onion, and finally garlic or ginger. The layers in the bowl will have the first ingredients to go in the pan on top. If you do not put everything in the right order, you will have to tip everything out and waste time.

When you cut vegetables with one of those ultra-cool Japanese knives, make sure that it is very sharp, but also that your fingers are folded in toward your palm.

When you butter a sandwich, do not leave the edges without butter.

Do not leave sharp knives in water. It dulls them faster. This also goes with graters and other objects with sharp blades.

Recipes

Just because you have managed to master a recipe does not mean it will turn out great every time. Variability always exists. Ingredients are fresher or less fresh, harvested near or far, and factors such as the happiness of plants and animals are unpredictable and wild. Accept this.

Do not be afraid to try out a new recipe on friends. If you cannot mess up with them, then with whom can you?

Do not follow a recipe to the letter. It is much more fun to experiment!

Always follow the recipe. Never invent or deviate from it if you are not experienced with that particular dish and those ingredients. Do not always believe everything the instructions tell you! For example, things may take longer to heat properly in the microwave than what is stated on the packet. This is particularly important when dealing with meat or shellfish. If you are not careful, you might give yourself very bad food poisoning not once, but twice!

Do not attempt to cook a Cauliflower Curry without the recipe. The resulting supper will be akin to the green sewage usually seen oozing from space monsters on *Dr. Who*.

Do not be a cookbook slave. Trust your imagination, and never think ingredients to be irreplaceable.

Do not believe a good chef has to present a new dish every time he cooks. You are a better cook when you also have a repertory of dishes that you are good at. Thus, arrange fifteen recipes that you like and get well versed in their preparation.

Do not believe the timings given in some cookbooks! If you do, your first Thanksgiving turkey might take an extra half day to cook.

Do not cook something more than two times.

Do not double up on your recipe without writing it down; otherwise when you get distracted—and you will—you will not remember how much you have added. The end result will be disastrous.

Do not exceed five ingredients in a recipe—you might enter into a hazardous, dangerous, and unstoppable experience.

Do not look at cooking programs on television for cooking tips and recipes unless you have a production crew living with you. However, what you can learn from these programs is how to look like a celebrity chef. Try wearing lipstick and hair products when fixing your next stir-fry. Talk to an imagined audience about what you are about to do. Prepare your ingredients and put them into small bowls, even if it is only baked beans in one bowl, butter in another, and slices of bread on a plate nearby.

Do not make the recipe exactly the same each time. If you do, you will never discover something wonderful. Maybe it will not be perfect one time, but the next variation could be even better. Only by learning to free yourself from following recipes will you become a half-decent cook, and that may be worth finding out about.

Do not not use a cookbook.

Do not put too much faith in the cooking times in cookbooks—it always takes much longer. Your oven is not as powerful as professional ovens.

Do not rely on your oven timer to tell you when it is ready. Ovens vary quite a lot, so do not set the timer according to what the recipe book tells you and forget about it. Keep checking and use your own judgment.

Do not start cooking before you have read the whole recipe.

Do not trust people who claim you cannot get a recipe wrong. You can.

If you do not remember exactly how your mother used to do a recipe, do not try anyway.

Do not try to cook a meal because you found it tasty in a restaurant without knowing all the ingredients used and the way it was prepared.

Do not try to make fudge entitled No-Fail Fudge even if it is a friend's sworn-by recipe. Do not get mixed up when making an inventory of the ingredients—or you will fail.

Face it, you do not have any professional cooking experience so do not try a lot of things you see on TV: chopping really fast, flipping things in your pan, and getting too creative. Just follow the recipe. Keep it simple and enjoy it.

For an important occasion, do not try a complicated recipe you have never tried before unless you have nerves of steel. Instead, practice your recipe again and again so that you can breeze through the kitchen effortlessly and leave your guests thinking that you are a truly gifted cook.

If you are planning an important dinner for a special occasion and really do not know how to cook, do not just try out a recipe from a book—the results can be hit or miss. This is not the time to experiment with new ingredients and new recipes. Stick to the ones you know you can accomplish.

If you are cooking a recipe with a lot of different ingredients or elements, cook them separately. Do not attempt the all-in-one-pot trick. For example, sauté your onions first, then add the garlic. Remove the onions and the garlic from the pan and use the remaining oil or butter to cook your meat, then incorporate the vegetables, and you will have everything cooked. Some vegetables release a lot of water during cooking and if you fill your pan with all the ingredients your meat will boil in those juices instead of developing a delicious crust.

Just because you have spent the whole weekend in the country with old country cooks showing you how to make Pesto with their age-old recipes and tools, this does not mean you will be as successful when you get home and try doing the same in your modern kitchen to impress your guests who have just flown in from a foreign country and are excited to try your cuisine. You might find yourself telling great stories to your guests about how the recipe was originally prepared, while they struggle to keep up a good face with your cheese lumps.

Never assume the recipe is accurately written. For example, measurements may be wrong, or they really want you to blanch the green beans but neglect to talk about the ice water bath.

Never follow online recipes. You cannot be sure of the author.

Never slavishly follow recipes; it makes cooking joyless. And never cook without love in your heart; it makes food tasteless.

Tarte Tatin, or so Raymond Blanc says in his introduction to his recipe, contains all the elements of pleasure—the dark caramel, the sweet and acid taste of the apple, the crisp pastry. To ensure you enjoy all these delights, do not use a pan that has a loose base. Use a solid-base pan and the caramel will soak into the apples—instead of the bottom of your oven.

When creating a new dish, remember that the overall flavor experience is not always better than the sum of its parts. Just because you like the taste of potatoes and of vanilla does not mean that combining the two will create a dish more flavorful and interesting than the two separate ingredients. Indeed, it is perfectly possible that the flavors will clash, and your guests will remind you of the flavor-failure that was vanilla-infused potatoes at every damned future dining opportunity, for years and years afterward, probably until death or even possibly afterward.

When having guests over for dinner, never stray too far from the recipe with the ingredients, in a clumsy attempt to experiment. For example, Brussels sprouts will kill any vegetarian Thai curry with its muggy smell. Replacing the chicken breast in a fricassee with chicken hearts because it looks exotic at the poultry counter and is also much cheaper—and after all you are a young student with little money—is not such a good idea, especially for a dinner date.

When making Hummus, do not forget that this is a free-form food enjoyed in a million variations by millions of people every day. Chances are, it predates the invention of the measuring unit that your recipe is written in.

Stop and think about when the recipe is important for ingredient ratios and when it is just a list of starting points to bang together something that meets your own preferences.

When making Semolina from scratch, ignore the instructions, as it will inevitably turn out to be too thick to stir. Just guess the amounts and be prepared to add more and more ingredients. When the pan starts to go brown at the bottom, and it will, do not think that it is done. Even if you turn the heat down, the browning will continue, appearing quicker than you can stir.

When preparing dinner for your friends, do not rely entirely on your creativity. Use a cookbook instead, or you will end up serving a strange milk pudding for dessert—flavored with too little sugar, ginger, and orange juice. If this is too boring in itself, do not add the mix of spices you bought in India two years ago. Your friends will wonder what it tastes like. Vegetables? Hemp? And they may remark: "My daughter would not have eaten this."

When reading instructions on a packet, make sure you check if the packet is open first, so that you do not tip it upside down and empty the contents all over the floor.

Do not disregard the recipe when you are not an experienced chef. Generally, the ingredients and instructions make sense regarding the outcome.

Do not follow recipes, unless for cakes. Experiment and learn by trial and error. You will love them like your own. And maybe others will too.

Rice

Never stop stirring a risotto, no matter how boring it gets, or it will not get creamy. Waiting time can only be cut out on TV shows—not in real life.

You do not have to settle for smoky rice. Add an onion until it is fully cooked. The onion will remove the smoky flavor.

Do not add salt to boiling rice if you have already infused it with stock. If you have, do not try to flush the excess of salt by rinsing the cooked rice—it might taste and feel like sea mud!

Do not burn the rice!

Do not cook rice too quickly on too high a flame—it will lose many of its nutrients.

Do not go and watch your favorite sitcom while having your dinner rice boiling on the stove. Do not even try to only take a quick look! Just do not!

Do not hurry a risotto by turning up the heat. No matter how much attention you pay to it and how much liquid you add, it will stick to the pan and burn. Risottos are boring to prepare and are meant to be cooked slowly. If you are in a rush try pasta instead.

Do not overcook pasta or rice. It sounds dumb, but rice is hard to cook!

Your dinner rice may be spoiled once you return to the kitchen after a commercial break. Do not even think you can eat the unburned parts. Just start all over again—and switch off the TV.

Do not try to cook rice without adding water. It does not work.

Do not use poor-quality fine rice noodles. It could turn your soup into a slimy glop.

If you are cooking Colombian-style rice and there is almost no water left, do not stir it. If you do, it will get sticky.

If you have fruits and vegetables you want to ripen, do not put them on a plate. Instead place them in rice. It is a trick to make them ripen very quickly.

Never put strawberries in rice, even if you want to change the flavor or color of the rice. The rice will always be too sweet.

Never stir plain white rice. Rather, use a rice maker instead of cooking it in a pot.

Never use long-grain rice to make a risotto.

Regular rice, contrary to risotto rice, does not need to be stirred more than twice. Do not stir your rice until most of the water is evaporated and be careful not to dry it.

Opposite to pasta, never cook a risotto in lots of water, on a high heat, or in a low pan for the following reason: The starch needs to STAY in the rice!

When boiling rice, do not add too much water or your rice will become mushy.

When cooking rice, do not be shy about the salt. When you think it is a little bit salty, it will turn out okay.

When cooking risotto, do not add too much water to the rice all at once. You do not want to drown your rice. Add the water gradually and keep mixing.

When you are making a lot of rice for several days, do not let your rice sit in water. The water will drain all the taste.

Salad

When making Honey Mustard Dressing with lemon juice, salt, and pepper, be sure to follow a recipe and its measurements correctly or you will just keep adding more of one ingredient to cover for the overpowering flavor of one or another, just to keep diluting them all with more and more olive oil until you have a whole bucket of dressing.

When preparing salad, do not cut the leaves before washing them or you will lose all the vitamins. Cut them afterward or they are really impractical to eat.

Do not add tomatoes to a salad. The water from the tomatoes will make the salad soggy. Instead, cut the tomatoes and serve on the side.

Do not cut lettuce with a knife, since it will break through its cells and lose precious vitamins. It is much better to tear it with your hands.

Do not cut salad greens with a knife; always tear them with your hands.

Do not cut salad into pieces that are too small—vitamins may get lost.

Do not dress a salad too long before serving it.

Do not put oil on a salad before vinegar, because the dressing will not stick well to the salad.

Do not put oil on the salad too long before serving it. Always wait until the last minute.

Do not think that it is impossible to burn the house down making a salad. Do not put an egg on to boil and go out into the garden to pick some vegetables, accidentally locking yourself out. Do not assume that others will be back before dinner and then decide to go to the library for a couple of hours, consequently forgetting about the egg. Do assume when you come back a few hours later you may find a fire engine and clouds of blue smoke bellowing from the house, and a pan that has boiled dry and melted. Avoid salad.

Do not wash lettuce in hot water—it loses its nutrients.

If you are salting salad with moist sea salt, and you did not break the salt apart while you were sprinkling the salt with your fingers, or if you did not toss the salad very well, you or yours may inadvertently consume a "salt bomb."

If you put a salad bowl on your stovetop, make sure the stovetop has cooled down, especially if your salad bowl is made of plastic.

Never season a salad while holding a cigarette.

When making a salad dressing with crushed garlic, oil, and vinegar, absolutely do not use mustard. Mustard is the poor man's garlic!

When making a salad dressing, do not add the salt at the end, because it will never dissolve. Add the salt first, then vinegar, then oil.

When making a salad with lots of ingredients, taste all the ingredients one by one. They all have to taste good. If you do not, you may find that one old can of corn will damage the whole salad.

When making a salad, do not dress it and leave it in the refrigerator; it will make it soggy. Have everything cut beforehand and dress the salad at the last minute or serve the dressing on the side.

While growing sprouts, carefully monitor them. If you forget, they become mildewy very quickly.

Salt 'n Pepper

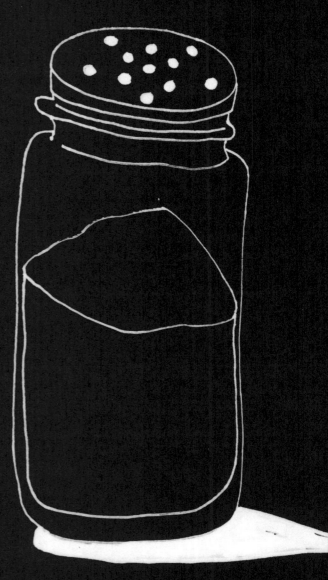

Do not add salt to a dish without making a public announcement to all those around you.

Kosher salt is great for a lot of things, but do not bake with it. When baking, use regular table salt, because kosher salt will not dissolve into the dough.

Always use coarse salt to salt boiling water, and never put it in before the water boils. A solute in a solvent raises the boiling point.

Contrary to what people think, do not put salt in unboiled water, because it will take longer to boil.

Do not add salt to the water when you are boiling corn, because the kernels turn into hard teeth.

Do not keep spices for years.

Do not oversalt the beans.

Do not overseason, do not overspice.

Do not serve unsalted butter to British guests.

Do not think that you cannot add too much coriander, hot pepper flakes, black pepper, white pepper, nutmeg, ginger, oregano, rosemary, cayenne, and turmeric to your dishes. You can never add too much cumin.

Do not throw salt into the water before it boils; the recipe may get salty.

Do not use all-purpose seasonings as a crutch. Learn how to use salt and pepper.

Do not use dried ginger for a spice. It tastes like curd soap.

Do not use salt at the beginning of the cooking process. This holds true for any type of dish.

Do not use salt without using anything else.

For making salad dressing, never add oil before adding salt. Salt does not dissolve in oil. For creating a nice smooth sauce, mix the salt with vinegar until it is dissolved and add oil at the end. Or replace salt with soy sauce, a nice alternative sometimes.

If someone is helping you cook, always ask them if they have already salted anything. This avoids unpleasant surprises at the table.

If you have a salt mill, never use it to salt boiling water. The steam melts the salt bits at the bottom of the mill, and when it gets hard afterward, your mill is encrusted and the salt will not be able to come out anymore. Cleaning it is a pain.

If you have put too much salt in your food, do not wash it under the tap.

Muscat must not be used in a fish dish. The tastes do not go well together. Muscat with meat is fine.

Never put salt and pepper on meat before you cook it. Salt makes the meat lose its water, and the meat will become tough—and the pepper will burn.

Seasoning a tortilla is very hard. If you use too little salt, your tortilla will be bland; use too much salt, and an inedible salty crust will form around the edge.

When dining out, always be sure to check which bottles are oil and vinegar at your table. A thorough check before drizzling on your meal will make sure you do not end up with slimy fish and chips!

When you suspect that you have not salted a dish enough, you have. It is always better to salt too little than too much.

Do not put too much salt in the pasta water. People will always want to add more salt to their plates without trying it first.

Corned beef and salt do not go together. The term "corned" comes from putting meat in a large crock and covering it with large kernels of rock salt that were referred to as "corns" of salt. This preserved the meat. Do not add extra salt or not only will you ruin your beef, but you may put your health at risk with all that sodium.

Do not put salt in your food while cooking. Let people add it later.

Do not use paprika powder in hot oil or butter. Only use after adding liquid; otherwise it turns bitter.

Lemon-pepper is gross. Do not use it. Do not think it goes well with everything, and do not think it will be just like lemon and pepper together. Use lemon and pepper, but never lemon pepper; it is MSG in a bottle.

When salting, do not pour the salt from the container directly into your pot without holding the salt in your hand. This cuts out the physical relationship between you and the food, and you are more likely to oversalt.

Salt 'n Sugar

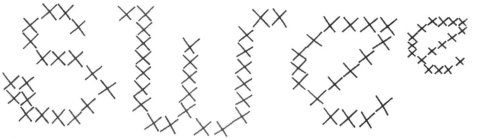

Do not try to make yourself more interesting by using salt instead of sugar in your coffee.

Although they look the same, sugar and salt are not the same—particularly when it comes to taste.

Do not keep your salt and sugar containers close together. The unintentional usage of one instead of the other in a moment of hurry can have dire consequences—or may lead to a new recipe!

Clearly label your salt and sugar pots. There will always be that terrible morning when you will not be in a state to tell which is which.

Do not forget to get out all of the spices you are going to be using prior to starting to cook or bake. If you do not, you may put chili powder on pies before noticing it was not cinnamon. You may ruin four pies this way until you learn to take out all of the spices you will be using and then put them away as they go into the dish.

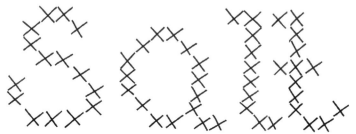

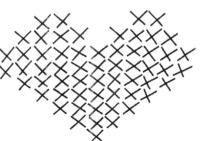

Do not keep baking soda, cornstarch—or any white powder, for that matter—in unlabelled containers, as you might think it is confectioners' sugar and decorate cakes with it.

Do not make assumptions as to which contains salt and which contains sugar.

Do not forget to label the sugar and salt dispensers to avoid salty coffee.

If you make Tiramisù, check that the pound of white stuff you put in is sugar, and not salt. If you bake twelve cakes at the same time, make sure that you do not misread a knife-tip of salt for a kilogram of salt. Salt does not go well in dessert.

When making an Apple Crumble in someone else's kitchen, do not mistake the jar of salt for superfine sugar.

Scotland

Do not despair. Nine out of ten shortbreads will always come out burnt.

Do not despair in times of economical need. During the war you could only get powdered eggs on rations in Glasgow. But if you lived in Ayrshire and had real eggs you could buy an unsliced loaf of bread, hollow it out, and put eggs inside to send in the post to your relatives in Glasgow.

Cooking disasters can happen even if you are just using a microwave. On Christmas Eve do not put a Christmas Pudding in the microwave for thirty minutes. You will be in the living room, thinking that there is a funny smell, and then you will go to have a look. The kitchen will be full of smoke, and you will have the doctor, the fire people, and the ambulance at your door. The cheeky devils will tell you that you need to take more care. From this point on, whenever the fire alarm goes off, people will say, "Is that you cooking again?"

Do not forget that not many people like Fruitcake. And so if you puff up with pride because you have baked a perfect Christmas Cake, you may end up feeling deflated. Beware, though: If you eat too much of the stuff yourself you may suffer from terrible colic.

Do not get drunk while you are cooking. Seriously, this was the subject of a whole TV public health campaign in Scotland.

Do not telephone the operator and ask him or her how to cook pancakes. They will not take to you kindly.

Do not worry if you cannot cook a half-baked meat pie properly. No matter how well you follow the instructions, they will always end up black on top.

If it is Christmas and the fan in the oven is broken, baking anything will be reminiscent of a helicopter hitting the crags at high speed. The broiler, however, might be working a little too well. The cold ham joint is on the table in all its glory, all you have to do is to toast the baguettes. The *Eastenders* theme tune is calling, you take your eye off the ball for a measly minute, and when you return to the kitchen—the scene of the crime—six black bread bullets like giant hamster droppings are lying at the bottom of the bin. You think the centers are spongy and can easily be saved, only to discover that the baguettes are partly baked.

Be careful what you wish for. If you are desperate to have fish for your tea, a colleague might go fishing up North, come back with some trout that you might pick the biggest of, knowing it is too big, and you might end up fighting for hours to gut it with a blunt knife while getting your kitchen bloody and ending up with a fish that is tasteless anyway.

Soon after moving in with your partner, if you are stuck for ideas for tea, do not decide to make Spam Fritters. This is something you will never repeat again or ever speak about, even after thirty years.

If you ever buy sardines in Sardinia, make sure you wash them before you eat them. They are set in salt, and when you pop one in your mouth you will get the dry boke.

If you take the notion to ice your shortbreads, do not do it before you put them in the oven, or they will come out with burnt faces.

When making a dumpling with clootie cloth, make sure that the piece of string tied around the cloth is long enough so you can use it to pull the dumpling out of the pot.

When making a light Christmas Pudding, do not use a dirty dish towel to immerse the pudding in the pot of boiling water.

When making a steamed Treacle Pudding, use self-rising flour. Do not use all-purpose flour, because after four hours of steaming, one made with all-purpose flour will resemble a disk of plaster of Paris soaked in syrup.

When making Mince and Tatties, be sure not to use coffee granules instead of gravy granules.

When melting chocolate for delicious Millionaire's Shortbread, do not be tempted to stir the chocolate, no matter how luscious it looks—it will go all lumpy.

When you cook a Haggis, do not forget to pierce the skin first to allow the fat to come out into the pan.

Do not scare your Haggis immediately prior to preparation. Frightened Haggii develop goose bumps with small clumps of acidic residue underneath, which in turn reacts on contact with Neeps. The reaction knackers your sauce, leading to the dreaded "Sassenach" situation.

When you warm up meals, do not start on a high temperature, and do not forget to stir with your Scottish porridge spurtle. Once you realize things stick to the base in spite of all the stirring, do not try to scrape it off the bottom of the pot—unless you want that certain flavor.

Sicily

125 PIAZZA ARMERINA
18 TRAPANI
2 S. LEONE
PORTO EMPEDOCLE 6

QUADRIVIO
PORTA ADREA

Casa Natale
LUIGI PIRANDELLO
Piscina
Communale

HOTEL
VILLA HOLIDAY

STOP

Do not fry pasta with marmalade.

Do not tell your grandmother you like something she made for you if you actually did not like it. She will make it for you over and over again for the next six months.

Do not take up with a Sicilian who cooks better than you do.

Do not soak bread in milk to make it soft and then add raw tomatoes and oil on top like they do up in Rome. This is like dog food to Sicilians.

Do not accept hard, chewy sun-dried tomatoes. Boil them with a little water for five minutes and add a bit of balsamic vinegar to soften them up.

Do not assume that Melanzane alla Parmigiana comes from Parma! Parmigiana is "Parmigiana" because in this dish the slices of eggplant are arranged like the shutters on a window. Parmigiana—in Sicilian dialect—means "window shutters."

Do not cook Carne di Crasto in a fancy villa on Via Roma. The grease will cover the ceiling and the floors for a week. Always cook it outside.

Do not cut the tails off of sardines when making Sarde a Beccafico or you will lose the imagined shape of the bird which poor people could not afford to eat in the first place, which is why they replaced it with sardines.

Do not fry anything when it is already hot! Perfectly fried food has to be cold from the start. Do not even think about frying a hot Arancine. It is not going to work, and you will not be the perfect Sicilian woman.

Do not cook fish with lemon.

Do not prepare Pane con la Milza late at night in your apartment.

Do not say you cannot eat well if you are poor. You can always stretch out a Caponata by adding some potatoes.

Do not use cream in Pasta al Salmone. Cream covers up the flavor of the salmon.

During a hot spring evening in Palermo, do not put dough in the fridge hoping that it will rise slowly. It will be transformed into a blob that is impossible to manage.

If you are poor and cannot afford thick slices of meat, do not despair! You can make your own meat slices using your meatball recipe. Cover the ground meat in breadcrumbs, but be careful when transferring it to the frying pan or it may fall apart.

Never add tomato sauce to Pesto.

Never make Sfincione at home, because no one will ever give you the right recipe. Everyone has their own secret recipe that they protect.

Never mix beans with meat, because beans and meat are both high in protein and are too heavy when mixed together. The only exception are fresh beans, like favas, and Zuppa di Fagioli con Salsiccia.

When making Focaccia, never confuse dried lavender for dried rosemary.

When making Pikkio-Pakkio, do not add onions or parsley, just garlic.

When making Pizza Fritta, do not cook the tomatoes. Leave them raw. Do not add a soffritto, which is the basis of all Sicilian cooking. Do not forget the oregano. Do not forget to put a little sauce on the bottom of the pizza before frying; it will make it a little softer.

When making Sicilian Cannoli, do not add the ricotta cream too long before serving or the shell will become soft.

When you come back to Sicily from Yugoslavia, do not try to imitate at home a simple dish that had been prepared for you overseas. Things that look simple to make are often not.

Do not call it Apricot Crostata if there are prunes in the Crostata and no apricots.

Do not put cream in the Carbonara.

Do not cook fish with lemon unless the fish is frozen.

Do not cook fish with lemon or salt. If you do, you cannot taste the sea.

For Pasta con le Sarde, always use bucatini grandi. Never use any other pasta—it is just absurd.

Never cook Baccalà with milk like they do up in Veneto.

Never mix fish and cheese—only when you eat Pasta con Brodo di Pesce.

Never serve Merluzzo cold.

Never, ever cook fish with lemon. Always add the lemon after.

Do not add too much water to the Panella. There is no room for experimentation in the recipe.

Do not cut Panella into thick slices, because it is served between bread.

Do not make Panella when you are in a rush, because you need to wait eight hours before cooking it.

If you want good Panella, do not talk while making the mixture. It becomes cold very fast and you will not be able to mix it after one minute.

When cooking Panella, do not put the mixture in the frying pan slowly.

Do not add oil to pasta water, except with tagliatelle and all fresh pastas. Fresh pasta is already a little sticky and tends to lose starch, becoming even stickier when cooked. A little oil will create a film around the pasta, ensuring that the pasta does not stick together. This is a fundamental rule!

Do not add oil to pasta water, except with tagliatelle.

Do not add oil to pasta water, except with tagliatelle and bucatini.

Do not cook Neonata. Just mix it directly into the hot pasta.

When draining pasta, do not pour out all of the pasta water. Save a little of the pasta water to add to the sauce.

Do not forget to add a little of the pasta water to your pasta sauces.

Do not forget to think about which pasta shapes go with which pasta sauces. For a very liquid sauce use a rigatoni or a penne, so that the juice can go inside the shape.

Do not make Pasta con i Broccoli using rigatoni.

Do not mix different-sized pastas. The only exception is Spaghetti Ministra, a poor man's dish, which mixes leftover vegetables in your refrigerator and all the leftover pasta in your cupboard. Do not forget, however, to check the cooking times of each pasta and add them in the proper order.

Do not overcook pasta. In fact, the pasta should be even a little tougher than you would like, because when you add the pasta to the hot pan with the sauce, the pasta will cook a little bit longer.

Do not put eggs and mayonnaise on pasta like they do in California.

Do not put ketchup on pasta like they do in California.

Do not use bucatini pasta for making Pasta with Anchovies.

Do not use farfalle pasta when making Pasta al Salmone.

Do not use long pasta for Pasta con le Lenticchie. Always use short pasta like ditalini.

Do not use long pasta for Pasta with Potatoes.

Do not use short pasta for Pasta con Olio e Aglio.

For cooking Pasta con le Sarde for large amounts of people, do not use any other pasta besides bucatini grande or penette.

Never put Parmigiano cheese on Pasta with Tuna and Tomato.

Never serve plain pasta as a side dish and put a big chunk of meat next to it like they do in England and France.

Never use fusilli lunghi to make Broccoli Pasta. Use spaghetti. Fusilli pasta with broccoli will be like glue. You must always think about how a sauce will stick to the pasta. Fusilli should only be used with thin sauces.

When making Pasta con le Lenticchie, never use farfalle pasta. It just does not make sense—the pasta is too big, the lentils are too small.

Do not serve Pasta alla Bolognese in the summer.

Never use beer in frying batter. Always use mineral water—the batter will be much lighter.

Do not add cream to a Ragù. A little milk is okay, but cream has a strong flavor that does not mix well with the Ragù.

Do not forget that basil is the secret to any good tomato sauce.

Do not forget to add a little sugar to the tomato sauce if the tomatoes are not ripe, because it will take out some of the acidity.

Do not put more than a pinch of bicarbonate into the Tomato Sauce. If it starts to foam or if you want to adjust it, do not ever add sugar. It is better to throw it away.

Never call a sauce Ragù if there is no meat in the sauce.

When making Tomato Sauce, if the tomatoes are young and not very ripe, do not add sugar to the sauce. Only use sugar when the tomatoes are very ripe.

Do not ever add sugar when making Tomato Sauce. If the tomatoes are not very ripe and are slightly acidic, add some baking soda.

Spain

Do not try to look super cool flipping your omelettes in the air, especially if you are using your last eggs.

When cooking a Tortilla de Patatas, do not let it stick to the frying pan, because you cannot turn it over. If the omelette sticks to the pan, it is possible that it will fall to the floor when you try to turn it over.

When cooking Tortilla de Patatas, do not peel the potatoes hours before cooking the omelettes in the pan—they will make the pan rust.

When making Bizcocho, do not forget to add the baking powder at the time of the mix. If not, when the mixture is in the mold and into the oven, the cake may not rise and you will not get a spongy and delicious texture.

When making Buñuelos de Bacalao, do not add too much salt when mixing with flour. Try it before adding salt, because bacalao must be soaked overnight and they cannot be eaten if they are too salty.

Do not break up your spaghetti before you put it into the water—you could offend passing Italians very seriously.

Do not take olives out of the jar with a metal spoon, only a wooden one. If not, they will go soft.

If you are making a Spanish tortilla and you want to reduce the calories a bit, bake it, but make sure to whisk the eggs first and then add them to the mix of onions and potatoes. If you do not whip the eggs, the tortilla will be flat instead of fluffy.

One thing is to cook like the Italians; another thing is to eat raw pasta. Do not overdo the al dente effect.

Perhaps they will seem graceful—so round and green on the yellow rice—but never put peas in a Paella; they just do not work.

This is cookery, not mathematics: The order of factors does alter the product. To cook a Paella, do not mix up the order in which things will be added. The meat goes first, the vegetables second, third the rice, and fourth the water.

To cook a good Paella it is necessary to have a Paella pan that is in perfect condition. After scouring it, do not forget to put a drop of oil on the pan before storing it. If not, it will rust.

When cooking a Paella, perhaps you may want to satisfy everybody, but, please, DO NOT cook a mixed Paella—for example, Chicken and Rabbit or Seafood Paella. To mix both options is tacky.

When making Suquet de Pescado or any other kind of fish soup involving a clay pot, do not use a pot that has even the smallest cracks, because the pot will make contact with the fire. The apparently innocent crack will cause the fish to meet the floor in front of your guests.

When you are making an omelette and you realize that it is sticking to the frying pan, do not try to use a spatula or a knife to unstick it. Just take it off the heat for a few seconds, shake the pan stylishly, and it will unstick.

When you make Banana Flambé, do not add the honey before you heat it up—it becomes toxic.

When I was a kid I remember that after cooking a Paella for exactly nineteen minutes, we would turn off the burner and cover the pan with one, or several, double pages of newspaper in order to let the steam finish the cooking of the upper level of rice that had been subjected to less time under the boiling broth. If you choose this ancient method, make sure that you do not use newspapers like *The New York Times* or similar, which leave ink on your fingertips. Otherwise, you will have an ink Paella. Instead you can use aluminium foil, but if you choose newspaper you can select pages with bad or good news, depending which mood you want to convey.

Splatters

Be careful when cooking with pressure cookers—they explode. Even if you are not sure why. If you are pressure-cooking carrots that are cut in small circles, they are likely to leave a polka-dotted imprint on the ceiling.

Do not put anything with beets in a blender and turn on the blender without putting the lid on and holding it in place while the blender runs. It will look like an axe murderer went berserk in your kitchen. Also, do not fill a blender more than two thirds full with hot liquid. The hot liquid expands in the blender and you can get BURNT.

Do not put hot soup in a blender. The lid may blow off and spray soup all over you and the surrounding walls and ceiling. Messy and very dangerous! Instead, leave the hole in the lid unsealed and cover with a tea towel.

Do not try pressure-cooking split peas for Split Pea Soup in a pressure cooker in the kitchen of a small restaurant in high-altitude Albuquerque, New Mexico, where your coworkers are also working to prepare the day's menu. The skins of the peas will get stuck in the pressure valve, and soon after an explosion will stop the hearts of all of your coworkers and yourself, while the ceiling, walls, floor, countertops, and your faces are instantly covered in hot, wet, green, not-quite-finished soup. Then you will need to spend the rest of the day cleaning up yourselves and the kitchen, while your customers wonder why their order is taking forever to come out of the kitchen.

If you put hot things in a blender, with the intention of making a sauce, do not lose track of how much stuff you put in it—or the blender will explode, resulting in wonderful and expressive sauce patterns on the ceiling. Make sure you secure the lid on the blender when making Beetroot Soup, or the kitchen will look like a scene from a massacre.

Simmering an unopened can of condensed milk in a pan of water for an hour or so turns the milk into the most delicious toffee. Do not, however, forget about the pan and allow it to boil dry. It will result in the can exploding and a ceiling covered in milky toffee.

When cooking Roasted Pumpkin Soup as a surprise for your housemate, remember to always hold the lid of the blender tightly closed. If you do not you will have an orange kitchen along with severe burns to the chest and hands. Always take good care with hot things, no matter how fun the color is!

Stocks

No matter how long you cook it that popcorn will never turn into corn in your soup.

A stock is only as good as what you put into it, so do not throw all leftovers in it like it is a compost bin.

When cooking a Caribbean soup, do not add the water you boiled your plantain in for extra flavor. It will make your soup black and disgusting.

Unless you like sweet minestrone, do not cook everything together. Cook the vegetables separately from the chicken broth.

Do not leave a soup on simmer and make lots of calls, or worse, go out. Your soup will disappear, and you will be left with muck.

Never believe that mixing two packets of Knorr soup will create a sensational and unique starter.

Do not add more than a cup of coconut milk to a pot of Creamy Carrot Soup; it may become too heavy and rich.

Do not forget that by adding lemon to your daily cocktail of fresh vegetable juice you neutralize all the goodness of the other ingredients. This same tip applies when cooking soup.

Do not forget that second-day soup is always the best. In times of hardship, like during a war, you may have to make dishes that will have to last for two or three days at a time. Soup is great because it is warming and filling.

If you make minestrone, avoid putting zucchini in it. This vegetable will suck up all the flavor and make it last less time in your fridge.

Do not leave any foam on top of the beef broth. Those are the meat's impurities.

Do not make a vegetable stock entirely from parsley, even if it is the only thing left in your garden.

Do not overload chicken stock with vegetables if you want the result to taste like chicken.

Do not stir Fish Soup or it will go cloudy. Do not cook it above 212°F.

Do not underestimate the power of fat. If there are rations in place during a war, you may only have an ounce of fat to cook with. If you try to make Barley Soup with that little fat, it may come out like wallpaper paste.

Do not use fish when you are making a broth.

Do not experiment with exotic spices in your basic chicken soup.

When making Leek and Potato Soup, or any potato-based soup for that matter, do not add those two leftover potatoes on top of the ones required for the recipe; this will only lead to a soup with the consistency of wallpaper paste.

When making noodle or rice soup, do not boil your pasta or rice in the clear broth. The broth will be cloudy, dull, and murky. It also tastes much better if cooked separately.

If you do not want salty Miso Soup, slowly add miso paste to your soup and do not forget to add it after the broth cools a little.

If you find yourself on your own after a long-term relationship, you may decide that a drastic domestic shake-up is called for by replacing convenience meals or take-aways with healthy eating. You may think that a large pot of homemade broth cannot be that challenging. After getting the basic vegetables such as leeks, carrots, onions, broccoli, turnips, potatoes, peas, and runner beans you may recall your mother making soup with barley in it. Do not think that putting the whole bag of barley in the soup will balance all the fresh vegetables. After bringing the concoction to a boil and turning the heat down to a simmer, do not go down to the pub for a couple of pints while it cooks. If you do, upon returning two hours later you will have quite a job getting the kitchen door open, as there will be a volcano of pearl barley erupting from the pot, over the cooker, down the worktop, across the floor, and jamming the said door.

If you intend to cook for your housemates, do not make a soup out of all the greens that were getting funky at the bottom of the refrigerator. The very same greens that, until then, everyone had been ignoring.

If you wish to cook a Pumpkin Soup for Halloween, when at the supermarket do not confuse the pumpkins with the jack o' lanterns, which look the same but make a greenish, herbal-flavored, possibly toxic soup that your guests will simply not forget.

Never cook fish stock for more than forty minutes; otherwise it gets bitter.

Never serve your husband burnt soup. He might miss that "certain flavor" the next time.

Never use the Wigeta brand to make a bouillon.

When cooking homemade Matzo Ball Soup, do not add chicken bouillon cubes for extra flavor without reading the label, because they often contain MSG!

When cooking instant Asparagus Soup with the declared quarter liter, do not put one package of soup into four liters of water.

When cooking Vichyssoise, do not substitute sour cream for the cream. These are not the same—and "Sourssoise" is not a dish!

When making a light, creamy soup, do not braise things too dark. The roasted flavor destroys the finer flavors you want to create.

When making a soup, do not just dump in ingredients. Think about it first.

When making a Sweet and Sour Lentil Soup, do not add the vinegar too early. The acid will prevent the lentils from cooking.

When making chicken stock, remember to put a bowl under the colander as you strain the precious liquid off the bones and veggies. If you do not, your stock will run away down the sink and all your hard work will disappear down the drain.

When making Egg Drop Soup, do not add any slivers of purple cabbage or purple onions. The purple pigment will turn the eggs gray, a very unappetizing color for eggs.

When making fish stock with shellfish, do not include the eyes from crevettes or prawns, because the stock will taste bitter.

When you are cooking a dish with a broth, do not add the broth at the end or your whole dish will only taste like the broth. Cook your broth at the beginning.

Substitutes

Bangers and Mash is not a tapas dish.

Always use the right type of flour. When cooking Victoria Sponge Cake for your wife's grandmother, do not use all-purpose flour instead of self-rising flour. The cake will come out flat as a pancake. You may not bake again.

Do not always put ketchup on everything.

Do not confuse condensed milk with Carnation milk.

Do not forget that to fail to plan is to plan to fail. If you are feeling that your Christmas dinner needs something extra, something to "funk up" the veggies and something for the missing "'x factor" that you are looking for, this will lead to last-minute desperate purchases being made to augment recipes, resulting in you heading down to your local twenty-four-hour BP garage and ending up with roast turkey stuffed with haggis, sprouts, mangoes, and moist chestnuts.

Do not presume you can substitute parsley for cilantro just because the leaves look a bit similar.

Do not substitute olive oil for eggs in a conventional brownie mix.

Do not substitute TVP for meat without adjusting the recipe.

Do not substitute vanilla powder for vanilla extract when making special Star-Shaped Biscuits. If the recipe requires vanilla powder and you cannot find it anywhere, do not substitute a whole bottle of vanilla extract for the powder. The results will be inedible.

Do not use olive oil instead of butter or margarine when making cakes, unless you want an acid edge to the flavor.

Do not use all-purpose flour when making pancakes; otherwise the pancakes will be like rubber bathmats.

Eggs Florentine cannot be improved upon by substituting tahini for Hollandaise Sauce. Tahini has no similarities with Hollandaise except an uninspiring hue.

For making mayonnaise, do not use a dominant extra-virgin olive oil. Only the very mild ones will work, which are rather expensive and hard to get outside of Italy. Any cheap oil like sunflower or corn oil will do the job as well.

If, for the sake of your slim figure, you want to try using yogurt instead of cream for a Cream Cheese Cake, be prepared to add gelatin and do not expect it to taste as good as the cream version.

If the recipe you are cooking uses butter, use butter and not margarine. Also, do not substitute Splenda or Equal for sugar, because it is not equal.

If you want to cook healthily, do not use margarine. The trans fats are unhealthy. Use oil or butter instead.

If you want to surprise your loved one with a cake, be sure to use real flour and not a baking mixture for bread instead.

In your first few years of cooking, you will see many substitution lists. You may even give a few a shot! Applesauce instead of oil, milk and lemon juice instead of buttermilk, whole-wheat flour instead of all-purpose flour. Unfortunately, the do-not-even-think-about-substituting list does not exist. Baking powder and baking soda are not interchangeable. Sour cream and clotted cream are not anywhere close to the same ingredient. And there is nothing—NOTHING—that can take the place of an egg.

It is not recommended that you substitute lemon juice with cranberry juice when making cookies that require just a bit of lemon. If you do, everyone will ask if your two-year-old brother made them.

It is okay to experiment in the kitchen, but think carefully before substituting ingredients and pay special attention to the implications of swapping A for B. For example, the following are poor substitutes: self-rising flour for normal flour, lard for low-fat margarine, ortolan for goose.

Never make Panna Cotta yourself, as it is difficult and the results are not overwhelming. Better to eat it in an Italian restaurant. If there is no Italian restaurant in your neighborhood, you might try to make Panna Cotta yourself at home. Do not use gelatin to make Panna Cotta, as it is made out of the bones of dead animals and might harm you and your family (crazy cow!). Better go to a health food store and buy agar agar. Get two liters of cream (the regular one, not the Weight Watchers substitute) and put it into a pot. Do not use a copper pot, as you might burn the cream and ruin the nice pot. Do not cook it on a high flame, as it might spill over and encrust the lovely range that you will then have to clean with soap water, causing rust. Add plenty of white sugar. Add the agar agar, which should not look like bonito flakes. Do not cook it too long, as the agar agar will get sticky. Let it cool down and serve it with caramel syrup. Hopefully there will be no grainy residue from the agar agar (that is totally not suitable for Panna Cotta), but after all it is made out of seaweed, and that is much better than meat. Meat is murder. If your friends complain, explain to them why.

Never substitute cornstarch with wheat flour when making gravy. The flour will go lumpy and ruin your dish. If you have already done it, put it through a strainer and enjoy it, post-lumps and all.

To ensure success in cooking, be careful with ingredients. For example, do not use sweetened soy milk for Savory Vegan Pancakes.

When assembling a dish that includes white wine vinegar among the list of ingredients, do not make the mistake of thinking it can be substituted with some white wine and some vinegar.

When attempting to make a Cuban-style dinner with Mashed Plantains, do not purchase plantains without knowing something about them. While black plantains will apparently mash easily like ripe bananas, green plantains will mash like a pile of wet woodchips.

When cooking chicken gizzards, never replace broth with the water you boiled the gizzards in. It is the most disgusting thing in the world.

When making Coconut Pudding, do not use coconut water instead of coconut milk or your pudding will be slimy instead of creamy.

When you have totally lost control over a dish, do not keep adding ingredients to cover up your mistake. Take a pause and then start over calm. If there are no more ingredients to use, order in.

NEVER add ketchup to a recipe that uses tomato sauce. If you cannot find time to chop the tomatoes and cook them on the pan, use a blender or a food processor to puree them. If you cannot do that either, buy canned tomatoes or the pureed version of it at the market. But DO NOT USE KETCHUP. It is never a substitute for real tomatoes.

If you are running out of yeast when making a Christstollen, do not use baking powder as a substitute. Recipes utilizing yeast must usually be allowed to rise before baking. If you mix yeast with baking powder, your Stollen will rise before, during, and after baking. It will not only look like a Christmas duck—it will also taste like one.

If you run out of ice, do not assume that frozen peas are a reasonable substitute, particularly for drinks that are not green.

Never use olive oil that is not extra-virgin.

CERVINO
MATTERHORN

MONTE
ROSA

Switzerland

When preparing a typical Swiss Raclette, make sure you place the heating plate of the cooker on the right side, otherwise it will burn your first-ever-bought designer table.

After having Cheese Fondue for dinner, do not have Chocolate Fondue for dessert—have something lighter.

Do not cook Cheese Fondue over the alcohol burner or candle alone; it will never get hot enough to eat. Cook it on a stove before transferring it to the burner.

Do not drink Coke when having Cheese Fondue. Have it with warm black tea or nice white wine instead. Both will help you digest.

Do not throw away the golden crust left on the bottom of the Cheese Fondue pot. It is considered a delicacy.

If you are doubling a Cheese Fondue recipe, do not double the liquid. Increase the liquid by one and a half. Otherwise, the fondue will be soupy, not thick.

If you live in Switzerland and you feel like cooking green cabbage, do not be surprised if you cannot find it anywhere. It is not popular there. You have to plan ahead and order it.

If you live in Switzerland, never try to cook with mushrooms out of cans or jars. No matter what sort or which brand—their chemical flavor will ruin your dish!

When preparing a festive dinner, one is usually advised to start early. This said, exceptions prove the rule. Swiss Cheese Fondue is such an exception where it is not advisable to start preparations too early. Even on a small flame the cheese will keep thickening. And if your guests are very late, it will have turned into a solid chunk of cheese by the time they arrive. You can still slice it and eat with the prepared bread. Do not expect much culinary praise for this, though.

When you make Cheese Fondue, do not ask your guests if they are lactose intolerant while serving it. That is definitely too late, and some people are too polite to say anything.

Toilet

Gentlemen

If your water supply is cut, do not stick your head of lettuce in the toilet bowl!

Do not stuff a turkey the night before. Guests apparently get sick.

Do not assume the tofu is still fresh. Ever. Always test it raw before tossing it into something. Always.

Do not cook when in a bad mood or if you are sad. It will make your guests sick to their stomachs. Besides, you are not going to be in the mood for entertaining.

Do not eat too much cookie dough when making your cookies or cake; otherwise you will get bad indigestion.

Do not follow your brother's suggestion to make Chocolate Orange Chicken by frying the chicken until brown, adding the chocolate, then the slices of orange mixed up and served on a plate. It will be a sickly mistake and your stomach will ache.

Do not forget that red cabbage is a very powerful laxative. Red cabbage soup will literally go straight through you.

Do not serve shrimp if one of your guests is allergic to it but does not know about it. He or she will spend hours in your bathroom and if you are lucky he or she will come back to the table—but with a very pale face.

Have you ever heard about Mithridates? If eating food after the date of expiry is a sport for you, do not forget how Mithridates died in suffering!

It is not advised to cook with leftover turkey three weeks after Christmas, unless you enjoy reclining on a porcelain seat for over five hours at a time.

Look over any shellfish very carefully before you throw it into a fish stock. Just one bad clam or mussel could give all your guests food poisoning.

Soups, curries, and bean stews all improve with age—they are tastier the day after you make them. But careful not to serve them too many days later unless you want to give your guests food poisoning!

To reduce the danger of food poisoning, do not use raw eggs that are too old for the Sukiyaki dish. Sukiyaki requires very fresh farm eggs to be beaten raw so that ingredients can be dipped in them before being eaten.

Do not trust a finger buffet. Even if your grandmother told you it is impolite to look inside sandwiches before you eat them, she probably never said anything about sniffing them.

When baking a cake, try not to lick the spoon that stirred the uncooked mixture. Raw eggs can contain salmonella, and salmonella can lead to three weeks in the hospital attached to a drip and being unable to change the TV channel.

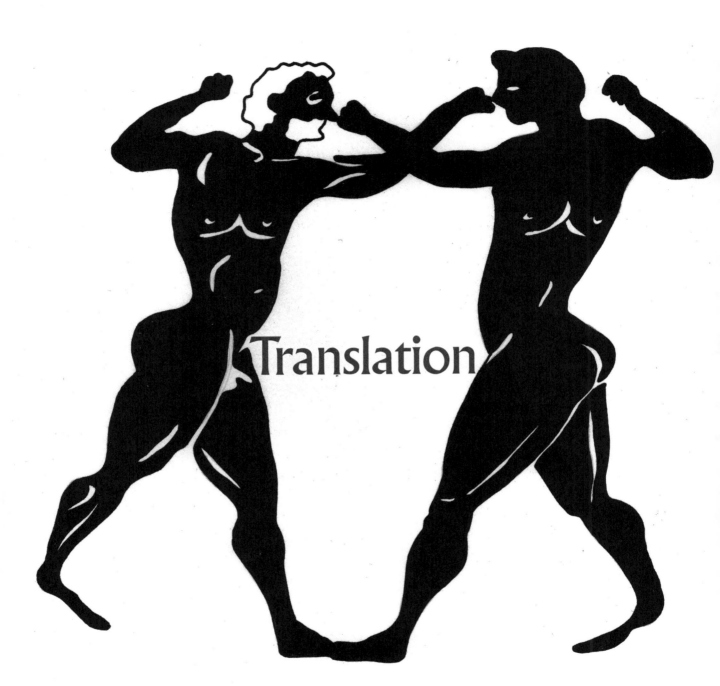

Translation

Never cook Bread and Butter Pudding for a Japanese person. It is, after all, just stale bread.

Always remember what size spoon you are using. Do not mistake a tablespoon for a teaspoon. This may end up making your cake taste like dishwashing liquid!

Be careful with red and white. Do not mix red and white wines, which, contrary to belief, does not make rosé. Do not mix red and white meats. In general do not serve white wine with red meat, or think of a good red wine for your white meat. Do not put white sauce on red meat, or sauce with red wine on white meat. It is only with the little red radish that red and white blend well together, but cooking red radish is actually a bit of a culinary experiment. It is excellent raw.

Before you try to cook foreign dishes, make sure the ingredients you are using are the right ones.

A Spanish omelette cooked with butter in England, or a pizza made with the wrong kind of flour, just does not work.

Crudités should be pronounced "crew-di-tay" and not "crud-eyes."

Do not assume that flour is the same in every country that you bake a cake in. It is not, and your cake will get a funny consistency. The same counts for foreign recipes that you find on the Internet.

Do not confuse measurement abbreviations, like "T" for tablespoon and "t" for teaspoon. It can really mess up a recipe.

Do not get muddled up between tablespoons and teaspoons. If you are a fairly undomesticated twenty-two-year-old and decide to copy your favorite recipes from your mom's recipe book, which includes a recipe for Chocolate Sponge Cake, do not make the mistake of copying "1 tspn of baking powder" as "1 tbsp." This will lead to an exploding cake.

Do not neglect to learn to pronounce the dish that you are preparing. For example: Spanikopita, Tortillas, Bouillabaisse, Bruschetta, and Confit.

Do not try to make Yorkshire Pudding in Canada. It does not rise with Canadian flour.

If you have a recipe in a foreign language, do not assume you understand all the words. If you get some ingredient or action wrong, the result can be horrible.

Just because your father was a baker and trained in Glasgow, do not think it will automatically make you a good baker. When you move from Edinburgh to the USA and try making Shortbread as Christmas gifts, you will have to find out how to convert grams to ounces. But as your recipe is in cups, you might mess up ounces to cups and end up with a tray of short bricks.

Never leave unattended any foreign friend while cooking garlic bread in tin foil, under the broiler, on top of a fat-full broiler tray. This is a recipe for disaster, especially when the said foreign friend does not know the emergency telephone code, panics, and turns to you to fight the fire, phone the fire brigade, and save yourselves and the cat.

When following a recipe, do not forget to make sure that you know what units you are measuring in, especially if it is a recipe from the USA that uses pounds, ounces, Fahrenheit, or any other strangeness.

When you first move to the UK from San Francisco, do not serve your husband a pint of cordial with his dinner without knowing what cordial is.

USA

Do not put marshmallows in your omelette even if there is nothing else in the house to eat.

Do not buy mass-produced frozen vegetables and microwave them in a casserole dish in three inches of water for five minutes.

Do not consider doing a cooking show where the ingredients seem suddenly prepared like in a Julia Child show. Do not use a ceiling fan as a food processor—it will be such a mess that hard hats will be considered a necessary piece of safety equipment.

Do not heat Pop Tarts in the microwave with the wrappers on.

Do not mix marinara sauce, refried beans, and ranch dressing. Even if you are broke and think it will taste good with tortilla chips.

Do not mix orange juice and milk together in an attempt to create an orange-flavored milk-drink known in the USA as Yo-J. It forms a precipitate. If you do, you should absolutely not put it in the microwave. It will smell like vomit.

Do not think you have to buy your produce at a supermarket. Instead, go to the farmers' market and make dinner with some of their fresh bounty—European style! They have great greens, which are always good sautéed with some garlic, olive oil, and chile flakes. You may discover that you love talking to the farmers and learning where your food is coming from.

Do not use butter in the crust when making Gravel Pie.

Do not, under any circumstance, decide that it is a wise decision to serve Frozen Fruit Casserole at a social event. Frozen Fruit Casserole is mayonnaise and canned fruit cocktail combined in a shallow casserole dish, frozen, and then served with a dollop of whipped cream.

Do not think that fruit stew, sometimes called Frew, is a good idea. A Frew recipe places a variety of fruits (such as apples, oranges, and berries), nuts (almonds, walnuts), yogurts (blueberry, peach), water, and cinnamon sticks in a slow cooker to cook for some hours.

If you do not add extra ingredients to a can of pasta sauce, like basil and garlic, you are not utilizing the full potential of the sauce.

If you want a cheese sauce, do not put cheese cubes and water in a bowl and microwave them.

NEVER poke a bratwurst; it will leak all the juices out. Midwesterners advise keeping a bowl of water near the grill while cooking bratwurst to dip your fingers in and rotate the brats by hand, no tongs and no pokey instruments. Wet fingertips only!

Pancakes require only a little amount of baking powder; if you overdo it they will be completely inedible.

When making Blueberry Pancakes, do not mix the blueberries into the batter. The batter will turn purplish gray and the blueberries will break, resulting in a mushy texture. Instead, you should drop the blueberries into the pancakes after pouring the batter onto the hot skillet.

When making oatmeal, do not quickly go to check your e-mails.

Whatever you do, do not cook like the English.

When a friend asks for your famous Pimento Cheese Spread recipe, neatly type out the ingredients:

8 ounces grated Kraft Aged Reserve cheese

1 small jar (4 ounces) diced pimentos, drained

1 cup Duke's mayonnaise

1 teaspoon sugar

Since it contains only four ingredients, the use of those ingredients, and only those, is obviously what makes the recipe so much better than any other. Do not use a sweet mayonnaise rather than Duke's, do not use a cheap, store-brand medium-sharp cheese instead of the Kraft Aged Reserve specified, and do not leave out the sugar. Do not forget to drain the pimentos. If you do not follow the recipe, do not complain that "It does not taste anything like the original recipe."

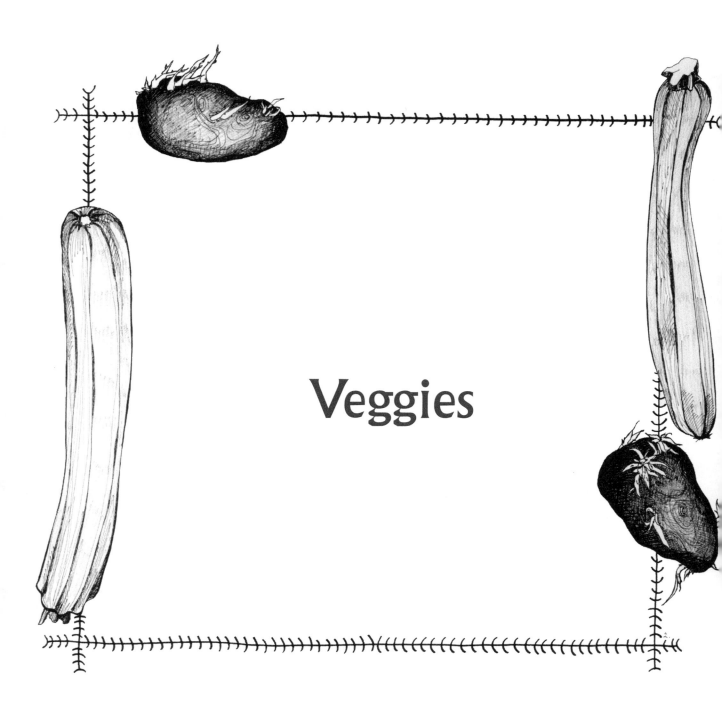

Veggies

Do not cook your vegetables until they are floppy and gray. Stop cooking them while they are still firm, lively, and colorful.

When you prepare a recipe with cooked tomatoes, do not forget to peel the tomatoes or the skins will roll up in strings that you will eventually find spread in your dish. To peel them off, just immerse them for less than a minute in boiling water. This will make the peeling very easy and fast.

Cooked avocados taste bitter and horrible, as do overcooked Brussels sprouts. For avocados, add them later but do not cook them very much themselves. For delicious Brussels sprouts, cook them Italian style with a little olive oil and salt in a small amount of water until just lightly tender and a fresh green color. Do not overcook them until they are soft and dark green.

Do not cook cauliflower without some sort of cover or they will oxidize. Actually, you do not want to use a pot lid. Instead, cover it with a wet towel. This way the cauliflower will remain white.

Do not dump frozen vegetables in a lukewarm pot of water. Do not think that doing so will be tasty.

Do not even try to bake a Vegan Pumpkin Pie with tofu, because the tofu will overpower the pumpkin.

Do not forget the cucumber. Cucumber Gin Cocktails appeal to everyone.

Do not forget to squeeze lemon onto the artichokes or they will lose their color and turn black.

Do not try to make 100 percent collard greens juice, because they are too rich in chlorophyll to juice on their own. Their juice will make you feel nauseated. Blend them with something milder, like cucumber.

Do not keep tomatoes in the fridge—they will lose their aroma.

Do not rush if you prepare a Cauliflower au Gratin. And beware of Tupperware. The little plastic monsters tend to develop a life of their own. Where is the light blue cover of the box where you are keeping the breadcrumbs? It is suddenly nowhere to be found. Then it turns up again, softly melted into bluish jelly, adding a remarkably artificial color and taste to the creamy sauce underneath the cauliflower. So again, do not rush; otherwise your family will not forget about the chemically flavored gratin, ever.

Do not slice beets before baking them; keeping them whole will keep the sweet juices inside.

Do not steam vegetables without putting water in the bottom of the steamer.

Do not wash mushrooms. Just cut the dirt off and wipe with a towel.

Do not wash the vegetables for too long before you cook them.

Garlic Cabbage is not a recognized culinary dish anywhere in the world. However, if you attempt to make Garlic Cabbage, do not cut up four cloves of garlic and one whole cabbage, boil together for one hour, and then serve on a plate without anything else. First, this is not a meal, and second, according to your guests, it will taste worse than a tramp's cock.

If you are using bell pepper for a sauce, clean the inside and remove the seeds. If you do not, it will make your dish very acidic.

If you want to avoid overcooking vegetables to make sure they keep all their taste, do not boil them—steam them instead.

If you do not like the smell of boiling broccoli in your house, do not forget to add a piece of bread soaking in vinegar on top of the covered pot. The steam of the broccoli, as it leaks out of the sides of the cover, will be absorbed by the bread.

If you do not put enough water in the pot for steaming vegetables or potatoes, the water evaporates quickly and the vegetables end up tasting carcinogenic.

When cooking Creamed Spinach, do not put the spinach together with the water to boil; instead boil the water first with salt. Once it boils, add the spinach. This way the cream will be bright green.

If you only have frozen vegetables left, neatly portioned into handy packets, do not assume these are boil-in-the-bag vegetables. While boil-in-the-bag rice may be readily available, there is no such thing as boil-in-the-bag vegetables. Vegetables prepared in this way will remain frozen. To avoid disappointment and broccoli ice-pops, try steaming them instead.

Never cook broccoli in cold water. Wait for the water to boil.

Never overboil veggies. They will look wrinkled and unappealing and no one will eat them.

Never wash mushrooms! They soak water like a sponge. Use a little brush to clean them of dirt.

Some vegetarians think that fish is a type of meat. Some vegetarians believe that cheese is a type of meat. Some vegetarians also have nut allergies and have a gluten-free diet. Some people are best not invited to dinner.

The tips of both green and white asparagus are the most delicious part—do not cut off and throw away.

When cooking for vegetarians, do not just cook what you normally cook—but without the meat. This is especially important when cooking Burgers, Lasagna, or Steak Frites.

When cooking green vegetables, do not let them overboil, as they will lose their color and will become grayish or dull. Instead, boil them for approximately five minutes or less and immediately place them in a bowl full of ice water. The color will stay as it is and you will have crunchy, shiny vegetables to nibble on.

When making a vegetable recipe, do not use vegetables that have been in your fridge for more than a week. The flavor may not be the same, and a light fermentation could happen in your stomach.

When preparing carrots, turnips, or asparagus, do not forget to peel before cooking.

When sautéing vegetables, do not forget to put the vegetables that take the longest time to cook in the pan first, such as onions and peppers. Then add the softer vegetables like mushrooms.

Do not overcook your vegetables.

POEM:

Hello Beautiful —
what are you drinking?
red wine for your
rosy cheeks or white
for your cold heart?

Do not brush your teeth before drinking wine.

Who is watching is desiring. Do not drink wine during the meal, because you may like it too much.

Never start cooking before you have a glass of wine. But do not start cooking when you are already having your second glass.

Do not put bottles of wine on the table. Instead pour the wine into a carafe with a large mouth so the wine can breathe.

Do not ever trash corked wine. Use it as cooking wine instead. The corked flavor will disappear when cooked.

Do not eat salad at the end of the meal accompanied by a glass of red wine.

Do not mistakenly add ground coriander instead of ground cinnamon to anything, especially mulled wine.

Do not add red wine to dishes with sausage—always use white wine. If you do not have white wine, mix a little water with lemon.

Do not put red wine in the refrigerator.

Worms

Maggots should not be put into the soup.

Before you stir-fry your wild mushrooms, make sure they do not have any worms in them, especially if your dinner guests are vegetarians.

Do not ignore the label saying, "Wash before use" on lettuce leaves. A slug in your Salade Niçoise does not taste good.

Do not insult your host by turning down food you have not tried before. If you are visiting the island of Samoa at the exact time of the year during the arrival of the palolo worms, your hosts will most likely serve these to you. The palolo (*Polychaete annelid*) is a rare and arcane creature with a transparent body that is green and wormlike. Similar to the habits of the California grunion, the palolo emerges annually from under the Samoan coral reefs. The palolos' appearance is determined by season, tide, temperature, and phase of the moon. Samoan chiefs and wise men try to determine the exact date and hour of their emergence. From your airplane window, you will already see the reflections of torch lights flickering on the waves, as fishermen attempt to gather up as many of the worms as possible, for they are a great gastronomic delicacy. The cooked palolo look like translucent green spaghetti Jell-O and taste like crunchy seawater. The morning after the meal, the villagers will carefully look you up and down and approvingly see that you have survived the banquet. After that, each night for a week, you will receive a heaping plate of worms. European (palangi) stomachs usually do not fare so well; accordingly, you will gain a little more respect in the eyes of the islanders.

During your one and only scout camping trip, do not take the initiative to make this recipe: one old Fray Bentos can, one hundred milliliters orange cordial, and slugs from a dry stone wall, heating it long enough to make yourself ill.

When having guests over for dinner, do not forget to wash the vegetables. This can help to avoid unpleasant caterpillars being found in the broccoli.

When making Poached Pears for a dinner party, try to remain sober before starting the preparations, and remember to check each ingredient before chucking it in. Otherwise, if you do not sort your larder regularly, you may end up with the unfortunate combination of pears marinated in Cointreau and slug pellets.

When serving lettuce from the garden, look obsessively for slugs and snails before feeding it to your guests. Do not forget this, especially in spring, when the slugs are very tiny, but active.

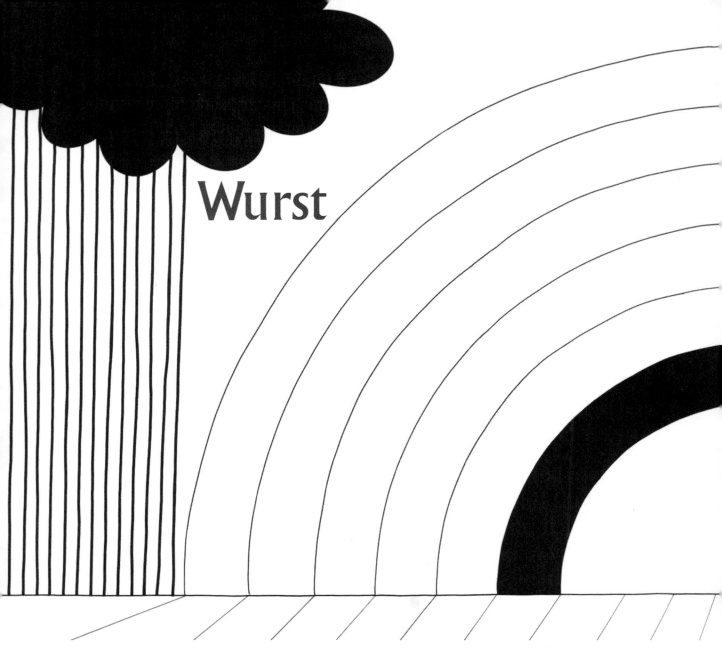

Wurst

When you are cooking wurst, do not use too much oil; do not make it too fatty. Grilling the wurst reduces the fat.

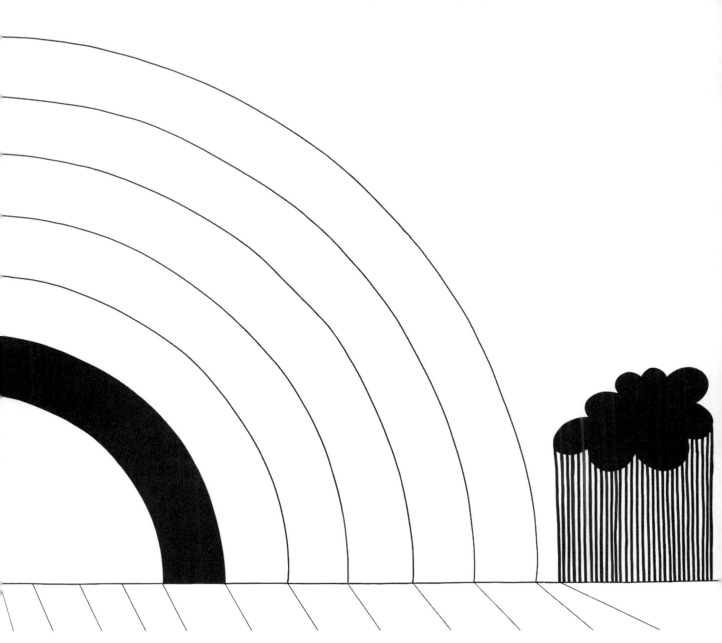

You do not want to leave your wurst for too long in the frying oil.

If a customer tells you not to put too much curry powder on their wurst, then do not put too much curry powder on their wurst!

Contributors

Anonymous	Anonymous	Anonymous
Anonymous	Anonymous	Anonymous
Anonymous	Anonymous	Anonymous
Anonymous	Anonymous	Anonymous
Anonymous	Anonymous	Anonymous
Anonymous	Anonymous	Anonymous
Anonymous	Anonymous	Anonymous
Anonymous	Anonymous	Anonymous
Anonymous	Anonymous	Anonymous
Anonymous	Anonymous	Anonymous
Anonymous	Anonymous	Anonymous
Anonymous	Anonymous	Anonymous
Anonymous	Anonymous	Anonymous
Anonymous	Anonymous	Anonymous
Anonymous	Anonymous	Anonymous
Anonymous	Anonymous	Anonymous
Anonymous	Anonymous	Anonymous
Anonymous	Anonymous	Anonymous
Anonymous	Anonymous	Anonymous
Anonymous	Anonymous	Anonymous
Anonymous	Anonymous	Anonymous
Anonymous	Anonymous	Anonymous
Anonymous	Anonymous	Anonymous
Anonymous	Anonymous	Anonymous
Anonymous	Anonymous	Anonymous
Anonymous	Anonymous	Anonymous
Anonymous	Anonymous	Anonymous
Anonymous	Anonymous	Anonymous
Anonymous	Anonymous	Anonymous
Anonymous	Anonymous	Anonymous

Anonymous	Anonymous	Anonymous
Anonymous	Anonymous	Anonymous
Anonymous	Anonymous	Anonymous
Anonymous	Anonymous	Anonymous
Anonymous	Anonymous	Anonymous
Anonymous	Anonymous	Anonymous
Anonymous	Anonymous	Anonymous
Anonymous	Anonymous	Anonymous
Anonymous	Anonymous	Anonymous
Anonymous	Anonymous	Anonymous
Anonymous	Anonymous	Anonymous
Anonymous	Anonymous	Anonymous
Anonymous	Anonymous	Anonymous
Anonymous	Anonymous	Anonymous
Anonymous	Anonymous	Anonymous
Anonymous	Anonymous	Anonymous
Anonymous	Anonymous	Anonymous
Anonymous	Anonymous	Anonymous
Anonymous	Anonymous	Anonymous
Anonymous	Anonymous	Anonymous
Anonymous	Anonymous	Anonymous
Anonymous	Anonymous	Anonymous
Anonymous	Anonymous	Anonymous
Anonymous	Anonymous	Anonymous
Anonymous	Anonymous	Anonymous
Anonymous	Anonymous	Anonymous
Anonymous	Anonymous	Anonymous
Anonymous	Anonymous	Anonymous
Anonymous	Anonymous	Anonymous
Anonymous	Anonymous	Anonymous
Anonymous	Anonymous	Anonymous
Anonymous	Anonymous	Anonymous
Anonymous	Anonymous	Anonymous

Anonymous	Anonymous	Anonymous
Anonymous	Anonymous	Anonymous
Anonymous	Anonymous	Anonymous
Anonymous	Anonymous	Anonymous
Anonymous	Anonymous	Anonymous
Anonymous	Anonymous	Anonymous
Anonymous	Anonymous	Anonymous
Anonymous	Anonymous	Anonymous
Anonymous	Anonymous	Anonymous
Anonymous	Anonymous	Anonymous
Anonymous	Anonymous	Anonymous
Anonymous	Anonymous	Anonymous
Anonymous	Anonymous	Anonymous
Anonymous	Anonymous	Anonymous
Anonymous	Anonymous	Anonymous
Anonymous	Anonymous	Anonymous
Anonymous	Anonymous	Anonymous
Anonymous	Anonymous	Anonymous
Anonymous	Anonymous	Anonymous
Anonymous	Anonymous	Anonymous
Anonymous	Anonymous	Anonymous
Anonymous	Anonymous	Anonymous
Anonymous	Anonymous	Anonymous
Anonymous	Anonymous	Anonymous
Anonymous	Anonymous	Anonymous
Anonymous	Anonymous	Anonymous
Anonymous	Anonymous	Anonymous
Anonymous	Anonymous	Anonymous
Anonymous	Anonymous	Anonymous
Anonymous	Anonymous	Anonymous
Anonymous	Anonymous	Anonymous
Anonymous	Anonymous	Anonymous
Anonymous	Anonymous	Anonymous
Anonymous	Anonymous	Anonymous

Anonymous	Anonymous	Anonymous
Anonymous	Anonymous	Anonymous
Anonymous	Anonymous	Anonymous
Anonymous	Anonymous	Anonymous
Anonymous	Anonymous	Anonymous
Anonymous	Anonymous	Anonymous
Anonymous	Anonymous	Anonymous
Anonymous	Anonymous	Anonymous
Anonymous	Anonymous	Anonymous
Anonymous	Anonymous	Anonymous
Anonymous	Anonymous	Anonymous
Anonymous	Anonymous	Anonymous
Anonymous	Anonymous	Anonymous
Anonymous	Anonymous	Anonymous
Anonymous	Anonymous	Anonymous
Anonymous	Anonymous	Anonymous
Anonymous	Anonymous	Anonymous
Anonymous	Anonymous	Anonymous
Anonymous	Anonymous	Anonymous
Anonymous	Anonymous	Anonymous
Anonymous	Anonymous	Anonymous
Anonymous	Anonymous	Anonymous
Anonymous	Anonymous	Anonymous
Anonymous	Anonymous	Anonymous
Anonymous	Anonymous	Anonymous
Anonymous	Anonymous	Anonymous
Anonymous	Anonymous	Anonymous
Anonymous	Anonymous	Anonymous
Anonymous	Anonymous	Anonymous
Anonymous	Anonymous	Anonymous
Anonymous	Anonymous	Anonymous
Anonymous	Anonymous	Anonymous
Anonymous	Anonymous	Anonymous
Anonymous	Anonymous	Anonymous

Anonymous	Agnes Wegner	Anna Palazzolo
Anonymous	Agustina Ferreyra	Anna Redpath
Anonymous	Aida Perez	Anna Reid
Anonymous	Al DeBolin	Anna Sottile Ciancimino
Anonymous	Alberto Nicolino	Annabel Bartle
Anonymous	Aldo Iacobelli	Anne Brennan
Anonymous	Alejandro Guzmán	Anne Fengler
Anonymous	Aleksandra Mir	Anne Murray
Anonymous	Alessandra Facchi	Annie Blocksage
Anonymous	Alex Farquharson	Annie Wu
Anonymous	Alexandra Ewenczyk	Annika Kristensen
Anonymous	Alexis Dirks	Anthony Galligano
Anonymous	Alexis Knowlton	Antje Majewski
Anonymous	Alexis Usuroff	Antonia Neubacher
Anonymous	Alfons Bach	Antonina Giusino
Anonymous	Alice	Archer West
Anonymous	Aliette de Fenoyl	Ari Feldman
Anonymous	Alison Currie	Arlene Sutherland
Anonymous	Alison Lee	Arthur Schneller
Anonymous	Alison Robinson	Asha Schechter
Anonymous	Alyse Emdur	Avital Sebbag
Anonymous	Amber Peel	Barbara Ann Mowatt
Anonymous	Amelia Best	Barbara Campbell
Anonymous	Andrea Merkx	Barbara Drover
Anonymous	Andres Mengs	Barrie Pottinger
Anonymous	Andrew Christine	Bella Reed
Anonymous	Andy Best	Ben Wilson
Anonymous	Andy Stillpass	Benjamin Fallon
Abdel Ouazy	Angel Montañéz	Benny Chirco
Abi Stuart	Angela	Bente Elise How Lode
Adam Coulson	Anja Lucht	Beverly Naidus
Adam Gill	Anjali Lockett	Bob Ross
Adriana Lara	Ann Tilley	Breeshey
Agnes Baumba	Anna Daneri	Brendan Jennings

Bridget Currie

Bruno Mayrargue

Camille Andrieu

Candace Watermeyer

Carlos Charlie Perez

Carmela Ice Cream

Caroline Kirberg

Caroline Schneider

Carolyn Burchell

Caterina Spina

Catherine Sargeant

Cathy Harvie

Chaveli Sifre

Chiara Baldisseri

Chiara Bombardi

Christa Dittmer

Christian Cummings

Christian Holstad

Christian Johann

Christian Roth

Christin Ripley

Christina Ballard

Christina Schwörbel-Binn

Christine Fremantle

Christine Scheuch

Cian Bell

Cindy Moreno

Cindy Ripley

Claire Mathijsen-Roth

Claudia and Arturo Ferreyra

Claudia Corrieri

Clémence Liffran

Col. Tacubaya

Colin Beattie

Colin Herd

Colleen DeBolin

Constance Chambers-Farah

Coqui Aguila

Cornelia Lauf

Cory Burr

Cristiana Thompson

Cyril Plangg

Cyrus Smith

Damian Killeen

Daniele Rossi

Dario Vitalezzi

Darrell Shines

David Calder

David Deane

Debora Wagner

Dee Rivaz

Denise Kauyedauty

Denise Mcdonald

Dhamayanthi Sangarabalan

Diana Cairns

Dimitri Daniele Perna

Dick Mernelia Randolph

Dirk Kinsey

Donna Holford-Lovell

Doreen Stout

Dorinda Ness

Eduard Carbó

Ed

Eilidh Crumlish

Eira Szadurski

Eleanor Pottinger

Elena Zini

Elisa Fiori

Elisabeth Karlsson

Eliza Wolfson

Elizabeth Woods

Ellen Babcock

Ellen Galligano

Ellen Rilley

Ellie Ga

Emily Arion

Emily Mast

Emma Ewen

Emma Macleod

Enrique Giner de los Ríos

Enrique Radigales

Eric Ferranti

Eric Legris

Erika Weinbacher

Esmeralda Morales Molina

Euan McDonald

Eugenia Viu

Eva Bühler

Eva Sangiorgi

Fiona Carr

Fiona Doubal

Fiona Fraser

Fiona Lee

Fiona Sutherland

Florian Bühler

Florian Christopher Seedorf

Francesca Ciancimino

Francesco Constantino

Francesco Manacorda

Francesco Pantaleone

Franco Ganci

Fred Emdur

Friedrich-Wilhelm Graf

Gabriel Rossello

Gabriela Camara Bargellini

Gabriella Ciancimino

Gabrielle Giattino

Gaby Dominguez

Gail Anderson

Gail Wight

Gaye Cleary

Genevieve Draper

Georgia Carbone

Georgia Kung

Gerda Warnholtz

Geri Loup-Nolan

Gesa Homann

Gian Paolo Morabito

Gillean Dickie

Ginger Smedley

Giovanni Ciancimino

Gisela Ruiseco

Giulia Lauricella

Giuseppe Giambertone

Gloria Perez

Gosia Wlodarczak

Greg Ford

Guido Litschko

Günther Brummer

Gustavo Domínguez

H. Wilson

Hamish Brown

Hans W Imbiss

Harrell Fletcher

Harriet MacMillan

Heather Dodds

Heather Richards

Hector Domínguez

Helen Brown

Helen Douglas

Helen Johnson

Helen Shin Lyu Abt

Helene Emdur

Helene McCulloch

Hermana Werlhof

Hervé Navard

Hilaria Molineros Salto

Iain Henry

Ignacio Hernando

Imke Wangerin

Ina Blom

Ingeborg Husbyn Aarsand

Inger Wold Lund

Isabelle Brombach

Isabelle Chen

Ivan Perez

Ivy Williams

J. Thompson

Jacob Peter Fennell

Jacquie Phelan

James Brook

Jan Coventry

Jan Killeen

Javier de la Torre

Jean Mclaren

Jeffrey Vallance

Jennie Guy

Jennie Prescott

Jennifer Brown

Jennifer Higgie

Jenny Richards

Jens Selin

Jessica Hakoun

Jessica Pooch

Jessie Lumb

Jim Williams

Jimena Cugat

Jimmy

Jimmy Sample

Joan Backes

Joan Macdonald

Joan Richards

Joanne Tatham

Joel Holmberg

Johanna Bussemer

John Barclay

John Calcutt

John O'Donnell

John Stevenson

Jonathan Goodacre

Jonathan Holmes

Jonathan Remar

Joolz Flynn

Jörg Heiser

Jorge Bravo

Jose Campos

Joseph Chiho Tang

Joseph Gibbs

Josué Calero Morales

Jude Hutchen

Juicy B (aka Michael K.)

Julia Dotoli

Julie Finkel

Julieta Aranda

Julio Suárez
Justin Carter
Kama Bentley
Karen Gory
Karen Remmer
Karin Schlie
Karma Lama
Kate Gagliardi
Kate Kernan
Katharina Fengler
Kathy Alberts
Katie Watters
Kay Lawrence
Ken Hollings
Kenneth Andrew Mroczek
Kerstin Schaefer
Khadija Zerrouk
Kim Cosh
Kristen Kosmas
Kyle Bravo
L. Clark
Lake High, Jr.
Lara Greene
Lars Sommer
Laura Barreca
Laura Getts
Laura Plumb
Lawrence Tooley
Leigh Adamson
Lena Maria Thüring
Lesley Wright
Liliana Lewicka
Lina Ozerkina
Linda Giusino

Linda Snyder
Lindsay Boyd
Lindsay Evans
Lindsay Jarvis
Lisa Anne Auerbach
Lisa Zeitz
Livia Corona
Liz Beard
Lola Greeno
Lorna Pirrie
Lotte Schâffer Andkilde
Louis Marchesano
Louise Kidd
Louise Smurthwaite
Lucienne Sencier
Lucy Guster
Luis Bisbe
Luis Lozada
Luis Macias
Luis Silva
Luisa Ortinez
Lynn Cowan
M.M. Dawson
Mack McFarland
Mae Johnston
Maggie Le May
Maggie Nesciur
Maggie Skinner
Maggie Tennant
Maggie Wilson
Mahala Le May
Mairi Gillies
Mairi Wilson
Maku Lignarolo

Marc Arpad Gabor
Marco Ganci
Marco Musumeci
Mareike Dittmer
Mareike Uhlmann
Margaret Hancock
Margaret McPhaden
Margaret Robinson
Margaret Robertson
Mari C. McCrossan
Maria Falconer
Mariana Guillén
Marie-Anne Mancio
Marilina Zaami
Marina La Manna
Marinna Wagner
Marion Black
Marjorie Walker
Marjory Beddows
Marjory Taylor
Marjut Börjesson
Mark Baker
Mark Fowlestone
Mark Gorman
Mark Le May
Mark Stauffer
Mark Wells
Marta Jimenez
Marta La Placa
Marta Munraba
Marta Muray
Martin Richards
Martine Rossello
Marxz Rosado

Mary Baker	Mor Germezi	Patricia Abeler
Mary Davenport	Morag Reid	Patricia Fyfe
Mary Knights	Muriel Hadden	Pattie Firestone
Massimo Gini	Muriel Pearson	Paul Fremantle
Matt W Imbiss	Murray Robertson	Paul Robertson
Matthew Curtis	Nancy Katz	Paul Steer
Matthew Wood	Nathalie Fiore	Pauline Adamek
Matthias Ulrich	Natz Spitsman	P.D. Rearick
Matthieu Laurette	Nick Hornby	Penny Calder
Maureen Lennie	Nick Shore	Petra Köhle
Maureen Stiven	Nicola Karcz	Philippa Elliott
May Smith	Nicole Belle	Pierre Bismuth
McCloud Zicmuse	Nicole Eriko Smith	Pierre
Megan Ohri	Nicole Miller	Pietro Leonetti
Megan O'Shea	Nils Cornelissen	Pilar Cruz
Melissa Laing	Nina Hien	Polly Jean Dance
Merryn Gates	Nina Kennel	Ray Harris
Miceli Alessio	Nina Siekmann	Rebecca Marr
Michael Arion	Nuria Faraig	Rebecca Steele
Michael Curran	Nuria Garcia	Reda Berradi
Michael Freudenberg	Olaf Stüber	Remi Emdur
Michael Ned Holte	Olga Berneburg	Renato Aracri
Michelle Souter	Oliver Euchner	Renee' Al Sheikh
Michy Marxuach	Oliver Herbert	Renee So
Mike Cruickshank	Ophelia Abeler	Rhea Plangg
Mike Turner	Ornella Cacace	Robby Herbst
Miki Suzuki	Oskar Holloway	Roberta Modena
Mima Benitez	Pablo León de la Barra	Roger Doubal
Mimi Kelly	Pam Arion	Ron Schultz
Mirjam Varadinis	Pamela Doherty	Ron Warren
Mirko Neumann	Pamela Erbetta	Rosa Leduc
Misu Paulus	Pamela Zeplin	Rosa Solá
M.K. Guth	Paola de Maria y Campos	Rosaura Diaz
Monika Aichele	Paola Pivi	Rose Nuhall

Rosemary Everett

Rosemary James

Rosie Cooper

Ruth A. Nicol

Ruth Fazakerley

Ryan Haley

S. Forson

S. Johnson

Sally Grizzell Larson

Sally Hansen

Sally Madge

Sam Lagneau

Sam Lohmann

Samantha Roth

Sander van Wettum

Sandra Linares

Sandra Peddle

Sandra Priebitz

Sara Bir

Sara LaBuff

Sarah J. Tingle

Sarah Martin

Sarah Mashman

Sarah Oakes

Scott Chaseling

Scott Keir

Seamus Clancy

Sean Carney

Sean Kennedy

Sean Watters

Shabd Simon-Alexander

Shaeron Averbuch

Shannon Davis

Sharon Siskin

Shilpa Baliga

Silvia Angileri

Silvia Rotllant Sola

Silvia Sauquet

Simon Howarth

Sonia Arion

Sonia Campagnola

Sonia Donnellan

Sonja Schepke

Sophie Darlington

Stav Fylachtou

Stephanie Wan

Stephen Hawkins

Stephen Neidich

Steven A. Stewart

Stuart Comer

Sue Prescott

Summer Hirschi

Susan Keys

Susan Macmillan

Susan Richards

Susan Rothchild

Susan Sakash

Susana Tarazaga

Tanja Blass

Tassilo Tesche

Taylor Hand

Tectonic Industries

Tere Recarens

Teresa Bravo

Teresa Callizo

Teresa Camprodon

Teresa Lucia Cicciarella

The Arion Family

Thomas Lambourn

Thymian Bussemer

Tim Dobrovolny

Timothy M. Ritty

Toby Webster

Tom Collins

Tom Holmes

Tommaso Speretta

Tonik Wojtyra

Trevor Wilson

Tucker Schwarz

Ulrich Best

Ulrika Jansson

Vaari Claffey

Valentina Monge

Valentina Nuara

Vanessa Cameron

Vicente San Juan

Vicente Todoli

Victor Dominguez

Victoria Roth

Walter Aprile

Warren Neidich

Wayne Bund

Wendy Davies

Wolfgang Oelze

Yitzchok Crawford

Yrsa Roca Fannberg

Yves Coussement

Yvonne Mullock

Contribute your advice to
The How Not To
book series

www.hownotto.info

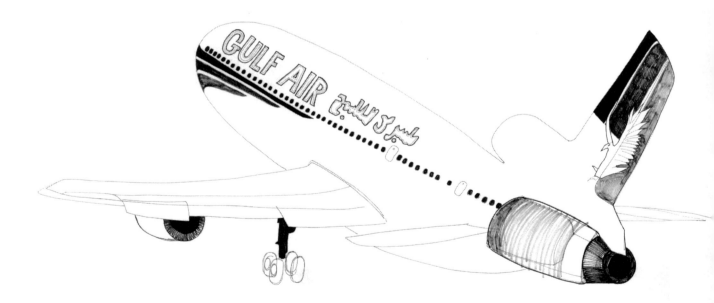